PEACEWEAVER

A Journey Through the Landscape of Difference and Indifference

---

Christopher Steed

Raider Publishing International

New York   London   Johannesburg

© 2009 Christopher Steed

All rights reserved. No part of this book may be reproduced stored in a retrieval system or transmitted in any form by any means with out the prior written permission of the publisher, except by a reviewer who may quote brief passages in a review to be printed in a newspaper, magazine or journal.

First Printing

The views, content and descriptions in this book do not represent the views of Raider Publishing International. Some of the content may be offensive to some readers and they are to be advised. Objections to the content in this book should be directed towards the author and owner of the intellectual property rights as registered with their local government.

All characters portrayed in this book are fictitious and any resemblance to persons living or dead is purely coincidental.

ISBN: 1-935383-83-3
Published By Raider Publishing International
www.RaiderPublishing.com
New York London Johannesburg

Printed in the United States of America and the United Kingdom

Acknowledgement

I have been in the company of so many great human beings who have both inspired and encouraged me on this journey, intentionally or unwittingly. Some of these have long since gone, including countless writers and thinkers, such as Emil Brunner, whose thoughts can be detected in Chapter 8. I am grateful to Gary Ward for the poem "Why?" in Chapter 42. But of living souls, it is Clare, who inspired the book ten years ago and who taught me much about peaceweaving, who deserves pride of place and a debt that can never be measured.

"The question is where humanity's daily meal of respect is going to come from. Official resources of respect have crumbled, leaving people to scurry back to old beliefs, and to nibble at new ideologies. The great religions grew out of a search for a meaning in life. The present-day movement for human rights, women's equality and the sanctity of the environment springs from the same sort of yearnings which the great religions tried to satisfy between twenty five and thirteen centuries ago. Respect cannot be achieved by the same methods as power. It requires not chiefs but mediators, arbitrators, encouragers and counsellors or what the Icelandic sagas called Peaceweavers, who do not claim to have a cure for all ills and whose ambition is limited to helping individuals appreciate one another." [i]

Make no little plans
They have no magic to stir the blood
And probably in themselves will
Not be realised.
Make big plans...deep into the future
Aim high in hope and work.
Have faith, remembering that a
Noble plan, once recorded, will never die
But long after we are gone
Will still be a living thing.

Goethe

PEACEWEAVER

Contents

SETTING THE SCENE
The Peaceweaver   1

THE FIRST LANDSCAPE
Denigration   9

THE SECOND LANDSCAPE
Depersonalisation   32

THE THIRD LANDSCAPE
Depreciation   58

THE FOURTH LANDSCAPE
Desecration   87

THE FIFTH LANDSCAPE
Dehumanisation   110

THE SIXTH LANDSCAPE
Demonisation   143

THE SEVENTH LANDSCAPE
Dedication   167

POSTSCRIPT
The Fiftieth Chapter   194

SETTING THE SCENE
The Peaceweaver

1
On and On into the Night

The Universe: its boundaries are uncertain, its limits limitless. If there is an end, what lies beyond that end? If one could sail to the furthest boundary of everything, what lies over the horizon? Have we reached the edge?

Some say that the universe is a giant sphere and to arrive is to have returned to the place from where the journey began. Others contend the universe is a hall of mirrors where the light is bent round, and what we behold is a reflection of other galaxies in the silent expanse in which we dwell or that we are unknowing inhabitants of one universe amongst many, and beyond the observable horizon lie silent multi-verses.

In a voyage of the imagination, leave behind mysteries that dwell in the outer limits of everything. Fly quickly past expanding galaxies and shrinking stars, past galaxies that are vast spiral nebulae and galaxies like Catherine wheels in a firework display. Leave Galactic super-clusters behind like lights along a motorway, each galaxy a metropolitan community of stars with many times more inhabitants than the largest cities on planet Earth. Flash past one hundred billion suns spread out over oceans of empty space, past beautiful Andromeda, the galaxy next door. Now we have arrived at the Milky Way. Star upon star rushes by. There is a spiral arm. Imperceptibly, we are being dragged round the heart of the galaxy on a journey that takes two hundred fifty million years. All human history could be comprehended within a tiny fraction of one turn on that stately circuit.

Speed past stars, countless stars and still more fiery worlds that toss and turn and roll in the night, stars that are like rain-drops on the windscreen at night, stars millions of times larger than the sun and stars that were smaller than the earth, star fields teeming, gleaming with blue flowers, red flowers, white dwarfs and yellow flowers like the sun, stars burning the candle fiercely at both ends, with a strange destiny of burn-out where stars are going out in a blaze of glory.

There was a medium size yellow star with a small family of orbiting planets, balls of gas or rock spending a million lifetimes in a frenzied dash around it. The third globe was a blue and white island. Descending through layers of a thin air cushion, the imagination glided gently down. On one of the continents a range of hills stood to attention above a throbbing city. As the Earth spun round, day had become night. It was a clear, crisp November night. On the hillside stood a tree, one of a number amongst a grove. In the tree there sat a teenage boy.

"Why is the world in such a hurry?" he thought. Was there a friendly face behind everything? Could he put a name to the face? "Is there anything out there that is like what's in here?" he asked himself indignantly.

In this lonely wilderness, the neighbours lived a long way off. What would it be like, he wondered, to stand on the edge of the universe, gazing into the unknown and the uncharted? We peered at the boundary fence and then a further expanse was detected that stretched into endless distance. The estate was never-ending.

He felt somehow that, despite the empty, inky sky, silent with the intensity that clothed the small hours of the night, he really did matter somehow. He stayed for a while, sitting in the tree, hearing the stars whisper friendly talk to his face until Aunt Freda called him in from the weaving she did at night to come and have supper.

2
The Perfect Storm and a Post-Modern Age

Many years passed.
Few saw the storm clouds gathering. The crisis, when it came, was a crisis of value, how much they were worth (not houses or cars, but people). Across the world, costumed with local dramas and global events, the gut instinctive value of these entities called humans had to be fought for with fresh vigour. Just when you thought it was safe to go back into the water! The machinery of the global economy, of terrorism, of difference and indifference, took ambiguous humans, discoloured them, drained their significance, and converted them into objects. And there they were thinking they had significance!
The financial system teetered and nearly crashed, like the house of cards it always was. Amidst a perfect economic storm, the likes of which had not been seen round for eighty years, savings, investments and companies battered and battered again. Six hundred thousand Americans a month were thrown out of work, banks and companies failed, and homes were carted off without fear or favour. In China, the authorities encouraged workers to return to the cities. They could not run the risk of the restless urban unemployed.
It was not just rich nations. Eastern Europe was starved of capital. Countries were going under. Ninety million souls across the world were threatened with forcible eviction into the desolate wasteland of extreme poverty. Human stock fell and fell again on the exchanges

of the world. In the wings lay the smirking spectre of extreme politics.

And still the dreaded devaluation did its unsightly work, remorselessly converting humans into objects. Many chapters were written; many wars fought, many victories won.

The 60's still exerted an iconic significance for those who were stirred by the heroic age of emancipation. Either that or the 80's had a magnetic lure to those fighting the culture wars and economic liberalism of that era of reaction. That was the day before yesterday. The General Staff was always fighting and planning for the last war. It was time for a new narrative.

By now, the third millennium was a good few years old.

On the threshold, humanity celebrated with parties to end all parties. The wine flowed, congratulations flowed, well-wishers endowed their fellows with smiles while fireworks; hugs and bells hailed in the new age. There were scenes in abundance set to dismiss anxieties and, amidst public rejoicing, eat drink and be merry. But, the full quote was left un-quoted; many songs were unsung, and the mood of festivity could not completely mask the inner trembling that crept out at the dawn.

The economy throwing a terrifying teenage tantrum, planes flying into skyscrapers, terrorists versus governments, war in the Middle East, dark clouds of human-doing warming and shrouding the planet in a hot burden of eco-concern: this was not how things were meant to be! For it was not merely with some sense of tension that humanity came to the new millennium; it was rather with fragmentation and longing. What people were longing for, few seemed to know. It was dismissed as nostalgia, caricatured as a fantasy of childhood, something needed to be re-captured. Pieces of a jigsaw begging to be arranged lay scattered for lack of a big picture to consult, and for want of a map of meaning, travellers stumbled on their journey. Everything was dissolved into compartments, but there was nothing to say what they were compartments of. The world lay broken into seared fragments of a tapestry, but no one could remember the lost tapestry or how to restore it. A vacuum yawned.

Old and trusted maps of meaning were yielding to the disorder of a fragmented world. In politics, in culture, in the economy, in technology, and in the shifting sands of human identities, nothing could be relied upon; nothing was certain. Slowly, western institutions and governments woke up to a shift of power to the East

TV image production dominated the air breathed. Artists were experimenting with radical new designs. A revolution was taking place in sexual morals and gender relationships. Intimate bonds assumed shapes and patterns that were always moving, rarely at rest.

The modern programme left the human spirit bereft, like an un-adopted orphan. Human concerns and ideals of love, truth, and honesty were split away from the real world. The world of science and the world of mind, spirit, and experience lay sundered in the dust. For three hundred years, the modern programme played endless variations on hopeful themes such as belief in progress and an optimism that rational, civilised thinking would straighten out a world rid of superstition. But, now the old narratives lay under a cloud of suspicion that they were power-plays in disguise. They still used the terms "left" and "right", but these were hackneyed and old-fashioned, fluid badges of convenience rather than banners to rally round. The old symphony of science, technology, and triumphant progress was still playing, but much of the packed gallery had gone off in search of another concert.

In the concert next door, everything became an item for consumption. Spiritual fulfilment drove the agenda. The map had changed. Fewer people were in church. Religion *seemed to bind people into doctrine, institutions, and rituals while spirituality connecting them to a journey of faith. Far more pursued a vagabond relationship with the stars. Beliefs and truths now had to be re-constructed by the individual using new tools of imagination and intuition. Hard and fast statements were replaced by story and symbol. Purpose was ousted by play, cold reason by warmth of emotion and spirit. A new consciousness was emerging where ambiguity and feeling were strangely at home with high-speed technology. In a post-ideological era, politics was dominated by personality and debates about method. Old answers were relegated to yesterday's news read by yesterday's men.*

Survivors looked out on a landscape that had changed. Everything was uncertain except for the certainty that uncertainty would prevail. Having jettisoned the old confident world, the loss was bewildering. Between new and old lay a great gulf over which played the sound of a lonely requiem. The distinction between this and that was washed away. Old male-dominated hierarchies lost automatic authority. Markers between fact and fiction, image and reality, past and present were eroded. One had to construct his own reality, make your own choices. Morality was what one felt one should do in a particular situation. Distinction between subject and object dissolved. There was no longer an external world to observe. Absolutes were over. The relatives came to stay.

What was this moment we had come to? They said it was a clash of values (plural). But it was more like a crisis of value (singular), the plural playing on the singular in a linguistic dance that was highly suggestive.

THE FIRST LANDSCAPE
Denigration

"We do not see the world as it is; we see it as we are." - The Talmud

"Someone who does not see a pane of glass, does not know that he does not see it. Someone who, being placed differently, does see it, does not know the other does not see it" - Simone Weil

"Without friends, no one would choose to live though he had all other goods" - Aristotle

1
Crossing the Gap

Dear Steve,

As I look back at the way life and journey coalesced at the beginning of the twenty-first century, it stands out how much progress has been achieved in the crazy struggle to assert our value in a bleak, unforgiving world. A movement of the brave is where it all began for me— a glint in the eye holding me in remorseless focus, sapping all other energies for movement toward the goal.

A goal, did I say? No, that cannot be it. That is too mechanical, too technocratic. A dream would be more accurate— a vision asking, "Why not?" You said last week that a global consensus could never come about, even for successful dreamers, even for pragmatic dreamers who combine what they see in the night with a healthy grasp of the possible. Nevertheless, possibility is transforming the world for me, and I continue in my journey with the same sense of adventure that we shared all those years ago. And yes, I am keenly aware of the wretched ambiguity this evokes.

I'm writing this email at Heathrow. The flight has been delayed by an hour, but I did want to say how glad I was to be able to have a good chat last week at Jack's funeral. It made me wonder how it was that we had ever woven that curious web of suspicion and mutual estrangement. But, I'm truly glad that that has long been brushed aside, that we could regard each other as people and greet each other as brothers.

That must have been the first time that we shook hands... ever! Maybe it took Jack's death to evoke deeper memories of when you and I stood at a memorial service for Dad, though there couldn't have been a funeral for him in view of what happened. Curious when you think about it that proper burials are a way humans have of respecting the dead, and by extension, the living, whether or not Jack deserved that respect.

Fortunately, I was sufficiently close by to mean that, in a little under forty minutes after hearing he had passed away, I pressed the door bell at the nursing home. I was shown into the room with Mum, surprisingly mobile despite her stroke. And there you were, along with Mandy, who sat in an armchair, looking at the fire. It was good to be brother and sister again, but I admit that she was a stranger to me then and at the funeral. Amanda looks fabulous, with hair that seems to dance like it should in a shampoo advert. She speaks freely. There's a buzz about her. When she talks about herself, her voice drops as if hiding a loneliness her mind doesn't somehow touch.

It was heart-rending to hear Mum wishing that she had gone to see him earlier that afternoon, as she often did; if only she had a memory of holding his hand. Those dark, grief-lined eyes! None of us knew what to say or do, though this was hardly an unfamiliar landscape. The mascara on her face was lined with tears like river valleys.

I was glad you were there and made the first move, the way you said "Mum!" with such feeling as you embraced and the tears flowed. For years, Mum had been waiting for that moment, but both she and Jack had put up too many barriers. Now, all the planned words dissolved. As we were never able to see Dad like that, wasn't it poignant to see our step-father with calm on his face that lent him an air of gentleness rarely expressed in life?

In those last few months, Jack knew he didn't have

long. Yet I was struck, as I always am, by the tenacity of the human spirit and a defiant unwillingness to be resigned to the inevitable. It is what I am coming to call "The Protest". The narcissism of self-importance as Freud characterised it? Or was it the sigh of "I count... I matter!"

From where I sat, I never felt I measured up, that Jack was indifferent to me. That feeling was a ghost that he commanded to walk the painful corridors of my mind. Until recently, I cursed myself, because he knew that I still craved recognition from a father-figure, but let's call him for what he was: my step-father, now old and frail. Forty years on, the ghost has finally stopped walking. I needed to make my peace with him before he died. He held out this limp handshake. At first it wasn't easy for me to take. What did I want with a limp hand? Afterwards, I was pleased that I had.

I don't know what passed between you and Mum when I stepped out of the room. I was glad to take in a little of the atmosphere of the nursing home where Jack spent his last days. It was certainly not clad with any sense of impending doom. Rather it was dominated by a lively group of old folk who had formed a cabal against death. After a late supper, a few old records filled the room with the light and colour of nostalgia at its best. There was some merriment, and they had a cup of hot chocolate. Matron cleared their cups away, a lady who breathed out an atmosphere of kindness and reassurance in the way that she treated them with dignity, unlike some nurses who keep asking the same question. She left them to it. A few of the staff casually joined in the songs as they breezed in and out of the room.

I watched for a few minutes as, in the dying hours of a December night, eight octogenarians exchanged their bittersweet memories of life. They were evidently protective of each other, their solidarity shining through in a brief encounter with someone who had just lost her husband. Their talk was of the times they had lived through that were now drawing to a close. They had seen three new generations. Scattered survivors of their own generation lived on. The darker side of optimism of when their parents were alive had been a fin de siècle era of decadence and a relentless search for anything that was new.

The cabal exchanged memories about where and when they were born, discussing what life had been like for them in those alien days when they lived on another planet. It was all there, so vivid, the day before yesterday. The flowering of childhood and adolescent years must have felt like the smell of awakening spring. I doubt if we would have felt like that after what happened.

Just then you called me back to the room to discuss funeral plans. But, I thought about that scene when I went to see Aunt Miriam to tell her the news. Wherever I go these days and get together with people over a drink or a meal, the conversation turns to the subterranean issues of life, the inner vision without which we are wandering listlessly in the dark. It's like there's a hunger that can only be acknowledged in whispers, a hunger to be heard and to matter somehow amidst a universe that belies our significance. I don't have all the answers. I'm still learning.

What I do have is questions. And I ask plenty of questions, to enquire what people are really thinking about their underlying concerns. Aunt Miriam helped me to recover when I hit the buffers, just as she did when Dad died. She casts her own particular brand of magic, turning her weaving into a metaphor for life. Her love of music is also pressed into service. She was intriguing.

"Listen to the music," she says. "Tune in to the themes playing deep down, and as the songs are heard, they will change in the hearing just as stories evolve in the telling."

That's why I've decided to leave my job as a counsellor and mediator in that North London community centre and travel a bit. I've got plenty of speaking engagements to keep me going following the success of my books. I have tried to help neighbours, families, and groups in dispute to learn to value each other so as to be open to each other's narratives. Maybe this will extend to a broader canvas in time. Who knows whether community action groups could ever become a partnership for raising the stock of human value at a local level? As Napoleon remarked, "Victory belongs to the most persevering!"

Now they are calling the flight, so I will touch base when I can.

Matt

2
Worth Every Penny?

It happened as he was jogging around Golden Gate Park before the meeting with the mayor. In this three mile antidote to the city centre, there came a moment of realisation, like seeing the punch-line of a joke, a light-bulb moment of insight in which sudden clarity brought a reaction. And as if the joke were extremely funny, the effect on him couldn't be contained. It was too palpable to dismiss. He felt as if he were suddenly implanted in his own body for the first time, pinching himself in amazement and laughing like a parent exploding with wonder at his new-born child, the latest cosmic creation. When he paused for breath, the Peaceweaver had an urge to laugh out loud.

"Just look at it. Look at what we have been given. Eyes, ears, fingers, toes, muscles! I can see, jump, walk, run, laugh, cry!"

Laughter and tears erupting from a group of children playing nearby made the Peaceweaver marvel that human thoughts were flushed with emotions. No computer could fall in love, feel remorse or be joyful like this. He felt the mystery of a new life fused together, a foetus dividing breathtakingly, into wonder. A human child was born, the result of nine months of silent, hidden sculpturing, enacting a programme for the formation of a unique person. Skilfully, mysteriously, the instructions knew when to build an arm, leg, heart, brain, skin, and bones. The hidden work had taken place in each of the million children who would be born before midnight. In years to come, today would be filled with birthdays.

He looked around him. To the east were the museums and the horticultural palaces, tea gardens, and bandstands. To the right were paddocks, arboretums, and thousands of trees running down to the Pacific. Joggers, cyclists, skate boarders, and strollers enjoyed the warm spring day, babies gurgled in their push-chairs, toddlers took their first hesitant steps, and children kicked a ball about. Teenage girls were being feted by adolescent boys, emotions and strange impulses rising for the first time. Without even asking, hormones were reconstructing their bodies, leaving them defiant and confused. In the hazy, lazy day, couples were walking, smiling or being cross, exchanging hard words or shy glances. People in mid-life were using the park and so were those who were ageing fast, whose bodies were wearing out. The body was, let it be said, a remarkable feat of design engineering, a complex piece of machinery with functioning parts enabling the occupants to grow and to go.

"We have bones, glands, muscles, and genes," thought the Peaceweaver, "but are we worth anything? There's got to be more to us than these amazing bodies of ours. Two thirds water, a pinch of salt, a brew of iodine, potassium, and chemicals worth a few dollars, and then mix enough iron to make a couple of rusty nails. Is that a human being? Is that all we're worth?"

He asked as he had a thousand times before, though now with new insight: "What is it about us that we can even ask such a question? How did the universe come into consciousness with this absurd notion that we matter? Does the universe value the end product? How did we come up with concepts of God, physics, trust, or love, or was it all the product of chemical reactions? Should we pinch ourselves, looking at each other to ask in amazement: 'Is there anything out there that corresponds to what's in here?' "

And he continued to jog around the park. "Hey, I matter!" he said to no one in particular.

4
The Interior Landscape

Dear Steve,

Thanks for your email. Sorry Liz had to work on the day of the funeral. I still recall when Mum told me that she had a letter saying that you had met Liz, another L.S.D. soul with beads, blown about by life, and you: a late arrival on the hippie trail, weary of changing the world. So, Ben is causing you grief. Tell me about! I haven't seen him since Mum's seventieth, but I well remember the encounter. He told me that he had seen my Daniel snorting cocaine outside a pub in London. I wish his Mum were still around.

That aside, things are going well for me on this journey of mine that is taking on a life of its own. It would be another universe to discern if there was a global consensus standing up for human value and the value of the world in which we are embedded, those con-joined twins. But, it would be helpful to use you as a sounding board for the thoughts and ideas that have been building up for a while. Let me know if that would be okay.

I've been trying to put into practice that piece of intriguing wisdom that I was given before I left. "Listen to the music," Aunt Miriam said enigmatically. "Listen to the music, and change the song!" There are certainly many songs out there with their loud thumping notes that you can't miss. But, the deeper you tune in, there are background themes playing that I'm endeavouring to hear and connect with. I'm becoming more and more convinced that you just can't understand the interior landscape without some concept of the struggle to realise our sense of inner worth and what I call "a valuable self".

I need hardly tell you, my own brother, how one particular landscape became familiar to me. You were there, too, an eye-witness. You will write with stern indignation and tell me that it was not so, but there can be no denying that you nabbed the first prizes at the school where Dad taught... And I? I was runner up at best, living under the greater glory of your academic shadow. Yet, though Dad urged us on always, his warmth meant that I was never made to feel that I was condemned to going through life second-class. There was no deficit where it really mattered.

But then, when Dad died, Mum married Jack and we all moved to Belfast, such certainties that I had possessed were then as ephemeral as a lingering puff from a steam train, imposing one minute, then gone with the wind. From that time, Jack worked overtime to make us fit in with his previous family. Do you remember how insistently he would urge upon us the only ethic he knew? "We can't have anybody around who is not one of us. You can do whatever you want. You'll go far. Build up a head of steam. No one can stop you. Show them all what you can do, whose son you are!"

It was dinned into me morning, noon, and night. My most enduring impression of Jack is a memory of a rather fat, bald figure puffing out his chest in the red armchair by the fire, sitting back in a haze of self-satisfaction and congratulation. I guess he had some cause. His business was growing quickly. Then came Sundays, and he would take us to Church, another opportunity to breathe out pleasure in his achievements.

At the risk of putting an emotional burden on an old man, now deceased, the sarcasm and the put-downs were arrows Jack used to devastating effect. I doubt if it came from serving in the Army, but he was a skilled verbal archer. An arrow? To me it felt more like he was an axe-wielding warrior when he got going. Did you feel this?

It's ridiculous. Why do we kid ourselves that we should feature at all when we hardly loom very high in the scheme of things? Maybe we are only the sigh of the universe.

The landscape of the mind is, after all, a site of ambiguity when it comes to human value. Some experience of devaluation is probably necessary to spur ourselves on or for human creativity. It was Nietzsche who said, "I say unto you, a man must have chaos yet within him to give birth to a dancing star."

Undeniably, put-downs can be amusing at times. My favourite is Samuel Johnson who said of Milton's Paradise Lost that it was a book easy to put down and hard to pick up!

All this is the stuff of human experience. I am recording not only impressions but also thoughts arising from people I have met or books I have read on my journey about the value of people and how that plays on the contemporary scene and in our lives. One struggle we often have is being belittled. It reduces us in size. We walk away from put-downs sawn down and smaller as a result or frozen under that icy indifference.

On another level, coming here has evoked many memories for me. When I was last here after the shock of losing Sara, I was just beginning to feel that, if only I could let go of the past, a vigorous, purposeful life would be given to me. I was like a boat adrift on a tempestuous sea. The old life was going to be shipwrecked. Old patterns would not work for much longer, though I would cling to them as long as possible.

An eerie glow wrapped enchantment around the moon tonight. I had to move quickly along the beach north of here or I would have been cut off by the tides, as if Earth was being rocked by the moon and water sloshed about helplessly. The human footprints still on the Sea of Tranquillity are embedded deeply in the imagination of my boyhood. That was before the troubles arose, Jerusalem, and with it, our tranquillity forever raped. The rush of memories moved quickly past me.

I recall the words of an old Zen Buddhist poem: "The world is dew... and yet... and yet." How can the spirit be kept intact in a place where everything is evaporated as the dew of morning? In the scheme of things, we carry no futile importance. To be involved with ourselves thus is to add delusion to collusion. Better if we did not feature so highly in our imaginary world and shrink away to a dot on the landscape.

Still no word from Daniel; it's an ache that I carry round with me like the war-wound Jack took at Arnhem. I'll send you the notes of a lecture that I gave in San Francisco at the psycho-therapy meeting.

Best wishes,
Matt

5
One More Straw and a Broken Camel

Uruapan lay in the west central highlands of Mexico. When the Spanish monk Fray Juan de San Miguel came in 1533, so struck was he by the River Cupatitzio and the lush vegetation it watered that he called the area "Uruapan": "eternal spring". Now the land of fruit and flowers had grown into a thriving city of two hundred thousand, a centre for the many farms that filled the district. An annual fair celebrated the quality and size of its avocados, an event incomplete without the regular bullfights.

The city had a strange attraction for the Peaceweaver from when he had gone backpacking years before and saw nearby Paricutin. It was still getting over one February afternoon in 1943, when an Indian farmer was ploughing his cornfield, and suddenly, the ground swelled, shaking, swelling and roaring steam dust. Within a year, a volcano rose above the surrounding land, buried in a sea of solidified black lava. Even now, the church tower in the village of San Juan peered uneasily above the black larva sea, a mute survivor of the day the Earth bulged and hissed.

At the Hotel Villa Flores, a colonial style hotel west of the central plaza, the bar was filling up. A People's Alliance? A movement of the brave? The community meeting had disclosed green shoots. But, now a growing crowd of people was pushing its way through to the front. The air was cloudy with smoke. Language and dress code aside, this could be any bar anywhere, replete with a generation looking without pause for love, who longed for real relationships and a re-creation the intimacy and community that, for some, was a fading memory. Relationships filled the human story.

In a quiet room, in a lunch-hour discussion, over twenty people gathered, an assembled group of those whose time to draw breath was shrinking and whose lives were furious wheels scarcely able to stop. The Peaceweaver reminded them that they were made for twenty-four hours to a day, seven days to a week.

"Have a day of rest. You can't do everything. Sort out priorities, but be sure to include time for reflection and prayer. Step off the pedal. Be more laid back. Take regular exercise. Make space for music or for reading to nurture your weary soul. Find slow lanes and times when you can go quietly and pursue a restful heart in protest against a world that is speeding up. Take time for people. Neglecting relationships is a sign of a burn-out.

"What is it about us that we have yearned for a completed life, to be enmeshed in a web of belonging? There are two patterns to the community we long for," the Peaceweaver said. "There are close-knit communities, where intimacy is a skill to be acquired, and there are communities with a task. To experience purpose without community is barren food for the human spirit."

And there in the corner was that Australian tourist. The cry of the lonely could hardly have been less in its anguished intensity. A great sadness crept upon him, stealthily as she began to open the storybook of her life, though she began at Chapter Five.

"I don't know why I'm telling you all this," she protested again and again. "The heartache of the broken is broken when someone listens. I need depth as I need water," she seemed to be saying, with pathos trembling in her voice.

"You are right," observed the Peaceweaver sadly. "What a gift to give to another when we listen to them, as if some food we had deemed luxury is after all our everyday bread. We need to be heard. Without it, our desolation cannot die."

"Why do I feel left stranded, like when a tide goes out?" she was saying. "Trust is built up slowly like a carefully made sand-castle. But, the tide destroys it with one destructive moment. We were made to belong; without it, we die. Fearing vulnerability, we are lonely inside our castle defences. Fearing commitments, we long for intimacy".

"Real intimacy will awaken you and light a fire to thaw out your coldness," replied the Peaceweaver. "But, there is a key that opens the door of cold, old castles. There is a need inside us that thrilled to be alive at the first flush of the world. But, what was sweet has turned sour."

The lips opposite were closed for a long silence. Then the lips moved. So, did her eyes.

"Tell me," she asked. "Why do we need others in order to receive the gift of being ourselves? If we have the ability to give value or to strip it away, we are then thieves and robbers and only rarely bearers of gifts."

"It is the Protest," pointed out the Peaceweaver. "This strange unaccountable sense of acting as though we have immense worth reacts against all its detractors."

She rose to get another drink. The Peaceweaver looked around him. Around a table in front of him, a group of young people collapsed in laughter. Pursuing relationships, they were engrossed in the circle of their friends. It was good to have friends with that special ingredient of picking up where you last left off without finding your way through the maze of a superficial relationship. Yet friendship, as with the mystery called intimacy, required the skills (and patience) for constant negotiation so that nobody's narrative should reign supreme.

The woman returned with another drink in her hand.

"I'm not going to be diminished a single day longer," she declared with vehement feeling that took herself by surprise. She had taken that diminishing deep into herself by inglorious self-appointment. For many years she held this status with hallowed memory and then grew weary of it. Her anger broke free with an eruption that rose from the molten core of her, and the Peaceweaver could only cheer with a contagious cheer that turned many heads. He left, rapt in thought, pensive though wanting to see with original vision. Was he catching a glimpse of how this internal motor worked?

"So does that mean to be empowered is to be valued, and to be disempowered is to be devalued? If that is the case, then are value and power brother and sister... or possibly identical twins? Is not to re-gain self-respect to re-capture power flowing back?" And with resonance in his own story, he realised the bonds of solidarity with someone fighting to assert that she was worth more than all worlds. That was worth a shout. And that was how a fellow-worker in Australia came to join the cause... and how a community began a journey to a spring, where green shoots were set to flower.

6
A Wing Shaped Piece of Shoreline

That Sunday, back in California for the rally in the stadium, the Peaceweaver went for a long walk along a wing shaped piece of shoreline that once lived near Los Angeles and, like an old beachcomber, had drifted to northern California. Francis Drake had landed there. Point Reyes was the epicentre for the earthquake ninety years before that had reduced San Francisco to rubble.

It was a drive of eight hundred miles since leaving Vancouver two days before. For most of the journey, winter sunlight bathed a coastline marked by rocky headlands, black volcanic sands, and giant redwood groves that defied the sky.

In the setting sun of evening, birds soared and danced, flaunting their untrammelled freedom with a boastfulness designed to impress the inhabitants of the flat earth. Suddenly, the Peaceweaver felt trapped, yearning to fly upwards and be lost amidst the blue heavens but held fast to the flat earth. Faintly, he heard music playing in his inner being. It was a song calling him to leave the restrictions of the horizontal world.

But, then a burning log distracted him, the remnant of an earlier picnic on the beach. The birds mocked him in their soaring, gliding movement. Chalk cliffs back-dropped a coastline, wet and windy. This place resembled the south coast of England, where he walked before the earthquake came. That was the real epicentre. His thoughts drifted to the beach where he went to school in Britain, where he used to stand watching the dredgers scooping muck and mud from the bottom of the estuary.

The Pacific Ocean roared at him, the surf crashing on the sandy beach. In the distance, he could make out the grey shape of migrating whales.

"What on Earth happened here?" he thought, looking at the scene around him. He shook his head again at the processes that shaped the landscape. Since birth, the planet had been dented, compressed, eroded, folded, faulted, split apart, and re-moulded. He knew that the world was not a peaceful place where landscapes were formed by silent procession. Planet Earth had a violent history, often being ripped apart. Titanic forces struggled for supremacy underneath them, storm battles above and battles beneath, waged under their feet. Awesome powers were on the move.

Nothing could be relied on. Nothing was firm. But that was also true of the solid ground. As a five-year-old, he had looked at an atlas and noticed South America and Africa fit together like one of his jigsaw puzzles. By then, science was waking up to the weird idea of continents wandering around! That was the day before yesterday. Today he stood on a living world.

He was grateful— profoundly so— for all the people who had sung into his life, for the songs and the faces that expressed those songs with welcome writ large.

But even as the Peaceweaver heard the noise of the repeated crashing of the tide, he was conscious of the sound that he was hearing from broken people pursuing broken dreams in a broken world. "Why do I live at the time of the breaking?" he wondered. "Why do my eyes see what I see and my ears hear what I have heard until I am blinded by the images and deafened by the blaring music?" He heard the sad notes of those compelled to build their lives on insecure foundations, crippled by inadequacy, fearful of new situations, insecure in relationships and clinging to a precarious foothold on life, as if barely holding on to a slippery mountain.

How many more ghosts would haunt the world! The Peaceweaver quivered in fury at the waste. The human tide continued to sweep over him. Sad and tragic music played on him like a CD that couldn't stop. He saw the stressed multitudes, visited with an epidemic of anxiety about the future— men and women everywhere for whom life was becoming intolerable, condemned like Sisyphus to drag heavy days around with them.

All this he felt, containing crowds within himself, standing alongside him, and he with them in resonant solidarity. The rally would be a Protest against the violent history of the world, people of goodwill finding common ground in the humanity that lay between them, despite the earth shifting beneath their feet.

And still the birds vaunted and flaunted their gliding freedom while the man on the beach felt a pang for his flat-earth life. Before, small acts of mental defiance seemed to be all he had. But, now he knew. No one was going to keep him from flying! And he would call others to join him in singing that birdsong amidst the landscape of indifference, in standing up for a valuable self that was worth more than all worlds.

7
The Need to Be Heard

It was as though he had been given a lens through which to view the world. The effect of how the value of people played on the contemporary scene stood out most clearly through its beckoning opposite.

In those days, he took up a lament. The song in a minor key played for those bereft of attachment, for the child in the womb, shaped not in an oasis of security but amidst a thousand discordant noises that pierced the primeval ocean with unease, giving indefinable sense of foreboding to the life ahead, for the little girl bombarding her parents with a parade of her achievements, hoping for recognition but beating in vain against the door of their attention, for the uncomprehending isolation of being cast aside at school, mocked and ostracised, not fitting in for she felt poor and plain, disappointed on the day when society handed out awards to the attractive, the rich, the intelligent, and the beautiful.

There was a young lad on that high-rise estate. As if being devoid of enervating experiences and food to stir the imagination wasn't constraining him enough, he had become accustomed to a verbal rough-house. His mother's flat was guest to abusive men, noise and trouble— always trouble— showing up in numerous disguises. She dwelt amidst nameless, faceless people, forced to dwell in a shrouded world covered by a mist of anonymity: heartless, lifeless and impersonal. A foggy world where neighbours rarely met, a key in the lock, hushed voices, raised voices, and a slammed door— nameless, faceless non-people living persistently in a world where all clung on wildly to believing that they were worth something against all the evidence.

Stress was the disease of the West; worry and anxiety were mass murderers. Psychiatric hospitals were full of victims broken under the strain. From ulcers to cancers, insomnia to alcoholism, the toll was heavy. One woman in two was depressed. Every other man was stressed. Extreme alternatives of fight or flight meant that they were kept on full nuclear alert without standing down, pepped up, ready to go. Psycho-therapy and psychiatry had to be recruited to preserve the mental health of western society.

This was how social evils were formed, layers of devaluation in different guises, people with problems conspiring in unwelcome alliance with human differences and all this operating together like some malign dual or triple computer processor.

There was that within everyone that sought a mysterious entity called "value". Everyone was compelled to live as if he or she secretly boasted significance, as if were worth something. Where that was absent, experiences of devaluation set up a reaction: that, at a profound level, I matter! But, experiences of devaluation created an energy that fuelled the Protest. Often, anger was hot collective indignation and the capacity for outrage a test of the bonds of humanity. "I'm worth more than that," led inexorably to, "We won't put up with this any more!"

He saw it in the constant but curious reaction people gave if they felt criticised. It was not just this or that action that was heavy with unwelcome scrutiny. They themselves were in the firing line; they, as people, were under the threat of verbal assault. So, they reacted from a different place, one that went to the molten earth core of them.

He heard the Protest amidst the icy blasts of cold indifference when someone was not heard, given attention or not consulted.

He heard the Protest when indignity led to indignation. "I'm worth more than that!" came up from somewhere, wistfully or volcanically.

He heard the Protest sighing from the denigration that left human souls reeling from encounters that reduced them to barely a metre high. It was into a house such as this— a reduced, cramped residence— that the latest put-down came to dwarf them yet again.

Everywhere there were deficits. Condemn them to live without value and the flowers perish, or they never unfolded. That they can still respond to the sun shows how essential that sun is.

Try as they might, the humans did not function well without a sense of a valuable self. They were condemned to live as if they had a value, to fight against the depression that was to lose the point of oneself. Self-respect or the value of significant others was not a self-indulgent luxury food. The language of their inner selves, where they constructed the meanings of everyday life, was clear: "Give us this day our daily bread!"

THE SECOND LANDSCAPE
Depersonalisation

"Attention must be paid, even to a salesman." - Arthur Miller, *Death of a Salesman.*

"You see, really and truly, apart from the things one can pick up, (the dressing and the proper way of speaking, and so on), the difference between a lady and a flower girl is not how she behaves but how she is treated. I shall always be a flower girl to Professor Higgins, because he treats me as a flower girl, and always will, but I know I can be a lady to you, because you always treat me as a lady and you always will." - George Bernard Shaw, *Pygmalion.*

8
The Riddler and the Riddle

It was the end of an April day, the kind of day that makes you feel summer has arrived. With the sun low in the sky, a crowd of people had gathered.

"The world is full of riddles," the Peaceweaver proclaimed. And he proceeded to tell a few riddles and do a few tricks. Nothing complicated. Just quickness-of-the-hand deceives-the-eye tricks. "But, I show you," he said, "the greatest puzzle of all." Slowly at first. but then gathering pace like wind brewing, he drew out a puppet, walking round and talking as he went. The puppet wore a female face that stared uncomprehendingly at the people. "What is a creature that struts and frets its way on the stage, leaving a litter of wounding words, wounded relationships and warring nations? Who is this mystery, so alive in consciousness, so aware of himself, the millionaire and the vagabond of the planet?

"There is a being that cannot come to terms with itself. Yearning to express itself but not wanting to be what it is, concealed behind a thousand ideals, harbouring innumerable contradictions in its inner being, unsure of where to go to be free from them or to untie the knot. Who or what is he?"

Some of the crowd stared at him. Others opened a door in their mind.

"And who is this who asks the question? Who is it, so conscious of wonder, so tortured with the lonely questions of existence? Who is this who even dares to pit himself against the vastness and claim significance? I show you 'the riddle and poser of riddles.'

"See this curious little creature: a citizen of two countries. Embedded in this world but relating upwards, seeking the other country from which she sprang; to which she will return. A little creature, forever seeking to find herself; forever fleeing from herself; forever drawn upwards, forever trying to release herself from the lure of the light, forever aware of inner contradiction, forever denying it."

The puppet put its hands over its appealing little eyes.

"But can we shut out the questions inside our head by blinding ourselves? Tormented by the unrest of continuing questioning, we are tugged by the immediacy of a connected life, haunted by the Eden-search for simplicity. Who will explain the mystery of why we are here or who we are or why we deceive ourselves into thinking we have worth? Who will solve the riddle of the being of value and maker of tools?

"But why is she a little creature? It is because she has been reduced in size."

The puppet looked doleful.

"Human encounters have lopped several metres off her stature. But still, she carries with her, in the teeth of indifference, acts of mental defiance that sing out a song of Protest. Now look more closely. She does not have a name. She is one of the nameless ones that inhabit our globe, a blue and white world where the personal and impersonal fight out a Manichean struggle with every passing day."

At this, to the horror of the audience, the Peaceweaver paused and proceeded to peel off the face of the puppet. All that could be seen was a blob of fluff where a face used to be. The audience gasped at such poignant audacity, and the Peaceweaver told a tragic story of nameless people who were looking for their faces. The puppet began to chase the face that had been lying on the floor as the Peaceweaver, playfully pushing it around with his foot. Would the puppet succeed in the recovery of its face?

9
On Canary Wharf

Dear Steve,

Thanks for your email. I am logging on here on Canary Wharf. I'm calling on a management consultant friend of mine to arrange a presentation at a seminar next month, but he's been held up. They say a sure sign that business is booming in central London is the number of cranes. So here I sit, in a time of recession, crane-spotting. Cranes to the left of me, cranes to the right. Is it twenty-eight, twenty-nine even? Not as many as there used to be.

As the world is slowly enveloped in darkness, the city slips into a different phase. Most formal work is winding down in the office block world that pierce the sky. Buildings of all kinds are silhouetted against the gathering night. But even as the lights are coming on, the city is coming alive with a beat and an excitement that is palpable. Out there, in the inky world, are restaurants and wine bars, cinema complexes, throbbing night clubs, and shops that stay open late. Somewhere out there, too, is my son Daniel living off the husks. I'd do anything to cross the gulf between us.

So, here I sit in the heart of corporate London, trying unsuccessfully to see stars behind the neon glare of night. I was, of course, wrong about planet Commerce winding down. It never sleeps here, and the people have to grab some where they can. It used to be called the "rat-race". Work should be for people, not rats. Corporate

Darwinism demands survival of the fittest: The best can grow; the rest can sink. This used to be a place where obscene amounts of money could be made... as long as you learn to lie, fit into the cocaine-fuelled economy or don't mind liquid lunches every day. And then the financial certainties exploded. All bets were off, and inky gloom descended on the city.

I was also wrong to idealise the scene around me. Not too far away, stretching away to the north, are tenement buildings that show that the other half is doing what it can to keep the spirit alive amidst unpromising surroundings and anonymous lives where real rats play and stay and where paint hangs off the walls. It's like high-rise land, those giant toasters piercing the horizon and besieging the community centre where I worked for eight years as a mediator and counsellor, doing my bit to empower the worst off and empower them to represent their own concerns and troubles.

So, Liz has been laid off work? She must have felt it after working in the factory for six years! That interview telling her the outcome of company downsizing was both unexpected and unnecessarily abrupt. "We won't be needing you anymore!" Small wonder she **was** too taken back to ask why they wouldn't be needing **her any** more. Inside, she must have been hollow with **deva**station. Passing the firm in the street every day couldn't have been easy. Not surprising she couldn't face it and cycled three mornings a week to the new play-group job by a longer route.

The lights of Tower Hamlets stretch away to the east. Last night, I met up with sister Mandy. She works nearby as a teacher and is still single. To her family, this is one of the great mysteries of life. You'd think that someone would have swept her off her feet long ago. I think Amanda enjoys keeping her distance, because if people get too close, they would reach into her inner being.

Mind you, some classes in her school are not easy. There are plenty of pupils with special educational needs. One of her children yesterday was permanently excluded. If the boy wasn't getting attention, he would disrupt so as to be sent out. He was failing his other classmates, and he knew it. He constantly referred to himself as "thick", his fear of being made to look stupid betraying inner chaos. For all the support Mandy gave him, it was a case of one disruptive pupil making it impossible for the others to learn. On recruitment, the head-teacher said that, if she could learn to teach there, she could do it anywhere. There are amazing teachers and inspiring episodes, the stuff from which heroes and heroines are forged. Half the community is white and thirty percent Bangladeshi. Apparently, four out of five excluded pupils are boys. The way to unlock the potential of disaffected boys is to give them value, they say. But, where is the source of such Eldorado gold?

I'm intrigued by the growing interest in learning powered by the enquiry of the child rather than knowledge being a thing we have to grab. There is a movement out there, an agenda which is beginning to recognise the value dynamic and work with it. As W.B. Yeats said, education is not filling empty buckets but lighting fires. Where children feel valued, they will do their best work. It is profoundly empowering to learn an instrument, chosen for the school play or the football team. It is feeding a latent sense of inner value. A child then weaves value around other areas of his life. Teachers, too, like pupils and employees anywhere, will do their best work where that's woven into school culture, obvious, though re-configured in a new way. It brings the best out in us though it is time to figure out why.

As I continue to listen to the music and hear this theme playing that will not go away, I'm quite convinced that human value is a vital lens through which to see the world. I seem to have struck a chord. At first it was just a website. "Peaceweavers" I called it, a phrase drawn from the old Icelandic sagas and Beowulf, in which someone in the community attempts to weave peace and help people learn to value one another. Then someone came on board, then another, then another, seeing it maybe as an antidote to the craziness of a world that persists in eroding the value of its people. Lots of people and social groups are engaged with this agenda implicitly. There are many Peaceweavers out there.

I am not after official statements and civil service replies. What I'm trying to do is build coalitions of workers, M.P.'s, business leaders, and teachers who can stand up against the ugly face of a world that devalues people. I seek people movements. Communities are responding, I think— men and women of goodwill daring to allow possibility to invade. I've come up with this phrase "creating environments of value". It's in the self-interest of organisations and societies to work with this value dynamic if they want to see their people be productive and contribute effectively.

There are so many encouraging road signs that tell us that we are making progress on the journey. I come across many schools where a commitment to diversity and equality is reflected in the atmosphere of the place and not just an item on the curriculum to tick off. In my local school, there was a staff training day that generated a poster describing ways that teachers sensed that they would be valued and therefore work more effectively. I cheered when I saw that. It's just up my street.

We've got to re-make the world one garden at a time. But constantly, you hear of management bullying or leaders who are deaf to their staff. Maybe it's what Schumpeter called "Creative Destruction".

I'm struggling to remember the name of the Economics teacher at Dad's school. Can you? He wasn't very good at crowd control. Not like Emerson, the Head. I found out years later that he had worked in Africa and had been involved in sentencing Africans in the bush. Maybe that was why he was a martinet. I know you were going to do Economics at A-level. Who knows? If events hadn't taken the turn they did, who knows? You might have ended up running one of those dot com companies or new media entities that are so numerous here in London now.

    Speaking of which, my friend has just arrived, so I need to log off. Talk to you soon.

10
Environments of Value

His work took him to India, an India that rocked and shone, replete with office towers and shopping malls. Even the facades of the garment factories of Gurgaon looked like three star hotels. Here, thousands of worker bees produced cars and scooters to stand in the traffic jams on the highway to Delhi. Here were the call centres, selling loan schemes to working-class people in the U.S. or asking people in the U.K. if they were happy with their energy and mobile phone suppliers.

"Tell me your story," said the Peaceweaver to a face in the crowd after he had spoken that day.

A name brought a face to life. Manilal had worked the land. Exported by the agrarian crisis, he now stitched and sewed for export.

"I work with a hundred others in a typical factory. It is a grave in a basement," said Manilal. "We cut, sew, and embroider. Then comes the finishing and packing. In the basement, the heat is heavy and solid, so solid that you can reach out and touch it. We have learnt to work with dust flying in the warm muggy air.

"Always, there is the smell, that sickly smell from the chemicals, that hangs over the basement and makes you retch. We have to buy water to drink. What choice do we have? But there is no space to eat inside the factories... Rent round here is high", he went on. "Who can afford it? So, most of the men live in the factories, sleeping on our mats. We work a twelve-hour day and get paid at the piece rate that barely buys food. Shifts for the women are only slightly easier. But, at least we have work. For that we are grateful. It gives us a job that our former lives in the countryside would not permit."

Asia's biggest Special Economic Zone was firmly in the making. Nevertheless, the Peaceweaver was insistent: "We must," he said, "re-define work or remain faceless and nameless in its pursuit. Too often, I have seen landscapes of labour in which the call to work is to become chained for a pittance. I have seen rats on the wheel in the West. Having joined the race, they cannot afford to stop. The wheel must turn faster, ever faster."

"Can it ever be any different?" they asked him.

"I will show you what work is and what it can be. To work is to create things of value", said the Peaceweaver.

That much was obvious.

"But what is the source of that value?" asked the Peaceweaver. "Some of it is in the land or ground, to be drawn upon respectfully and as stewards."

"Some of it is in money" added someone quickly. "And that is the source of our problems from those who exploit us."

"Blessed are the risk-takers," observed the Peaceweaver. "But the value lies not in the ground or in the bank. It is within those who come to the enterprise and bring their labour."

Was that not obvious also?

"But consider," urged the Peaceweaver. "To work is to take the value that is within us, within our story, a worth that cannot be measured, to create things of value that can be measured. You have heard that it is human capital that is crucial."

The eyes of his listeners seemed to glaze over.

"Those who organise, those who manage, and those who own take the value that lies within those who labour, and behold, it is converted."

His listeners woke up a little. Could they see their work through different eyes? If so, what would that mean?

"You who labour have it within you to weave your magic— a brand of magic that is peculiar to you— upon the raw material in front of you and to turn it into gold!" insisted the Peaceweaver.

Now that was alchemy worth possessing, his hearers pondered.

"To see our labours in that light is to shroud them with the sari of recognition," said the Peaceweaver. "To discern that we ourselves are the source of our work is to elevate labours that have dignity without recognition— bringing up children, emotional labour in caring for others, and creative tasks— and place them alongside labours that have recognition granted by others. It is to personalise our work, to connect with labour that evokes our value without treading upon it with rude heels. It is to distinguish work from work and exclude all that would demean and destroy others, for that casts dark shadows over work rather than bringing it into the light."

They all knew about that. They had seen the exploiters of children and of women, the drug-pushers and the gangs that populated their landscape. They remembered the debt collectors in the villages, joining the queues of the labourers.

"It is to sound a Protest against landscapes of labour that devalue. It is to declare to impersonal forces and faceless people who run things: "We will not collude with your face-denying, name-removing acts. We are recovering our faces and our names!'"

"To those who organise and those who manage, I say this: Your task is to create that which can be valued from the labours of those who work with their hands, their heads, and their hearts. Go and create environments of value, landscapes throbbing with a surge of energy as the labourers draw on that which is within them.

"Devalue them and the link between inner worth and outward output, between being and doing, is severed. Give self-respect, personalise their work and your reward will be the best powers that are placed at your disposal for a while. Here is your challenge: Nurture the value of your people. It is from there they will draw out what is in them. The connection between what we are and what we do is most fully realised where inner worth is nurtured and released. Then we will create outcomes that are worth much. I urge you: Help to re-image the human landscape - one garden at a time! Help the people recover their faces!'

12
Workplace Wars

Dear Steve,

I'm really sorry to hear that you are having a difficult time at work. Having a boss that never consults and displays such indifference can't make for an easy place to work.

These days, it's bad form to attack someone for what they are or to make personal comments. That's come to be considered rude and outrageous, but it doesn't stop it from happening. This type of constant undermining can make the workplace very grim. I guess you'd agree. It never ceases to amaze me how many managers like yours fail to award value to their staff beyond the monthly pay check.

By the way, Mum told me something recently I didn't know about our late, lamented step-father. Apparently, Jack lost his own mother when he was four. He couldn't remember anything more of her than the shell-like existence to which he was condemned when, for the most part, he had to bring himself up. He was plucky, too. Evidently, he was captured at Arnhem and spent the next few months in Germany before escaping. All that made me see him in a somewhat different light.

Nevertheless, it was to Jack's disappointment that I found myself drawn to psychology rather than business studies. College, university, research in psychology, a few unsuccessful attempts at business, lecturing— then breakthrough! Head of human resources in a genetic engineering company! For years, we had watched academics in America escape to start biotech firms. Most of the venture capital still went to American firms. Europe didn't succeed in producing a rival to Genentech.

Genetic engineering: wonderful. A bright new dawn, utopia on the next train. This was to be the cutting edge. But, I was unprepared for the cut and thrust. I thought science and research was bad enough. There's a great myth in science. Scientists tell everybody else that they are driven by strict objectivity. What they don't tell you is the mud and blood on the carpet. They leave out the reaction against new ideas or the infamous battles of like the huge rift - valley size quarrel over those hominid finds in East Africa.

I thought all that was bad enough, but I was unprepared for the cut and thrust of industry. Senior management had scant regard for people who didn't understand the technical end of the business. Meetings were marked by disdainful comments and those knives that were ready to be dug in and twisted into your back. "Why do they all need knives anyway?" I used to say in naive disbelief. You shared impressions with people you thought you could trust and build alliances with, and it would be all round the tracks the next day. It was like the Labour party!

It can be hard work indeed if you know that your colleague doesn't respect your work, but every time you bring something up, it's your fault. And your boss chimes in that you are not showing the same attitude as you used to! In those corporate conditions, people look to their own interest first, then to the interest of the company. Warped by competitiveness, they focus on the task in hand and don't think wider.

There was a problem. I won't bore you with the details but I had a very tricky issue. My colleague was perhaps responding to fear but everyone took his side, including the Senior Management Team. What struck me rather forcibly then was the human need to be taken seriously, not to be treated as a piece of rubbish. I wanted people just to hear. I banged the door and the walls and everything else in sight. Instead the shutters were down. It never felt like I was meeting a real human being, just someone playing an impersonal role called "Managing Director". It was frankly hard to adjust to the new position that they had made for me. I was heading for the buffers. The stress mounted. While I was busy trying to win at work, other areas of my life were as neglected as my garden at home. Tired and weary inside, at times, I felt that I had nothing else left. That was magnified a hundred times by the inability to get the company chairman to allow my voice to pierce through the enveloping fog.

 I resigned. In that fog, I had lost a great deal of the purpose and self-esteem that I had re-built. There I was, at the age of thirty five, out of a job and out of an identity. That atmosphere of denigration with Jack was added to, with compound interest, by put-downs in the workplace. I knew instinctively that all was not well, that life was troubling me deeply, leaving me bereft of a sense of feeling worthwhile. I could no longer quieten the Protest, those involuntary utterances of mental defiance, a Protest gathering like mounting debts, to be resolved sooner or later. You have to drive on automatic for a while.

 In that time of meltdown, I turned my psychology degree to good use, re-trained as a psychotherapist, and began to practice while lecturing at the university. My private practice kept things ticking over financially. Disadvantaged people at the community centre didn't really pay the butcher! The secret knowledge of despair had qualified me in a way nothing else could. "Turn your wounds into gold," Auntie Freda told me.

 We all recognise the restorative power of recognition... and it's opposite. We can dance away on the idea that, in the scheme of things, we hardly matter at all. And yet... and yet... and yet! We demand to be respected, to be taken seriously, to be given dignity. Dignity at work is now seen to be necessary food. Where there is encouragement, we thrive. Where people can't make their voice heard, or where the company won't listen to their needs, organisations shoot themselves in the foot. It's against their self-interest and very short sighted, as they could be more productive.

What seems crucial is to create a space for a story to be heard. There, different voices can meet. Instead, ears become closed, needs become demands, and voices become shrill. Stories that are not told solidify. Unheard and unnoticed, we are devalued.

Do you wonder why, if not consulted, you often walk away feeling flattened? And then if you are given a worthwhile project, you realise it's not a personal attack and your confidence builds. Its core stuff. It's the motor of human value humming away in the background. Wise leaders who listen to the music are sensitive to these dynamics.

I'm glad for all his being a right so-and-so that Jack received care and dignity at the end. You hear of many experiences that people have at the end of life, where they are stuck on a ward when they'd rather be at home or when busy nurses, rushed off their feet, don't listen or greet them in any meaningful encounter. It's too de-personalising.

I experienced in myself the other day a reaction against impersonal forces. When the Building Society was taken over, they re-jigged the account numbers. My internet banking facility was in trouble, as the ID was wrong. Could I get through to someone to sort it out? For ages, I was passed from electronic pillar to post, trying unsuccessfully to outwit the robotic forces. Eventually, the humans won, and I got through to an actual person! It was sorted in ninety seconds. Humans 1- Robots 0!

The other day, a Mayor wrote to me with an idea. How about trying to promote a city-wide agreement people could sign up for, a kind of covenant in which we will join forces to fight against all the ways we devalue others. This is, after all, an agenda so many people are working toward either implicitly or explicitly. Surely, we couldn't build a world where the old devaluation and relegation was for the history books. Yet when groups of all colours sought to mobilise public opinion in the U.K. about a Climate Change Bill, they nudged 100,000 responses. That's people power!

Time to go.

Matt

13
A Tale of Producers and Consumers (and the Three Marketers)

"Once", said the Peaceweaver, "some people who lived long ago decided that they wanted to make lots of money by making things. These were the "Producers". They became very good at it. Factories were created where work could be concentrated, mechanised, and powered by the black gold of coal. Now that they were not working in their homes, the workers could no longer see the result of their labours. At first, the Producers only knew how to create factories where long hours of back-breaking labour could be undertaken amidst grime and smells and where the labourers lived in cattle sheds. It was bonanza time.

"But another group was forming, a group that created the demand for what the Producers had to offer. They were the "Consumers".

"The Consumers were delighted with what the Producers had to offer, who in turn created more and more. They were locked in a dance on a spiral staircase. However, what was left out of the equation was that the joy was in the acquiring of objects. The heights of satisfaction did not last long before the inevitable fall off and return to base-line happiness.

"The workers, who had to spend a lifetime under gruelling conditions began, to resist. Exploitation was a song of Protest at first whispered, but then the unrest grew louder. The workers were treated as cogs in a greedy machine in a mechanised age. Socialism, unionism, communism— let's challenge the system or abolish it altogether! But, the revolution was postponed. An invisible hand took the labours of Producers, even as they struggled to keep wages low and profits high and generate a common wealth, enough at least to keep the workers simmering in the border country between contentment and discontentment. And the analysis of revolution and exploitation had a fatal flaw that only really emerged in the remedy proposed. Those with fire in their minds did not anticipate that the new rulers of a worker's paradise would end up devaluing their adherents and devouring their children. Neither did they see that the useful energies of the workers would be stunted, not released. They concentrated on sharing wealth around but had no answer to how to create it.

"The approach taken by the Producers began to be extended to more and more types of work. Everywhere, the demand was for more, more, more in ever increasing varieties, shapes, and sizes. The Producers cracked the whip, demanding ever increasing output, output, output. Scientific management became fashionable. Workers were given smaller and smaller bits of the machine to work with. For many, this was the chance to earn. For most it was tedious drudgery softened by a monthly pay packet and the camaraderie of the canteen. Workers became extensions of the machines.

"Workers fought the conditions in which they were expected to work. Men and women bolted to the factory floor for so long, dehumanised, were rising up in indignant protest. Something about the way human beings were made had been ignored. To keep up, companies were obliged to make the wheels spin faster and faster. Its workers on the treadmill had to run just to keep up. Then assembly lines were dismantled. It was the Protest.

"As time went by, the Producers tried to ensure that every enterprise pursued vigorous value for money. It was not all about factory labour. Multiplying status was to become the elixir of life to generations of professionals, anxious to achieve recognition. The world of health and education began to be affected by the tireless demand for output, output, output, measured by performance and results. No area of human expertise, welfare, and work was left untouched. The cosmos was being run by accountants, aiming at the markets, selling units— always units, units and more units.

"To entice people to buy the products of their ingenuity that flooded the markets, the Producers enlisted the help of the Persuaders. The Persuaders formed a group of Three Marketeers: swashbucklers all amidst heroic scenes of print, film, and electronic media. And so, advertisements acquired sophistication amidst the flickering images of television. The Three Marketeers led. They determined the images. Everyone else followed.

"Fiercely competitive amongst themselves, the Producers had to sink or swim in a larger pool. Everywhere, local Producers were faced with the tidal wave of global markets.

"But in the melee, something had happened to the Consumers. Locked in this dance on a spiral staircase and calling the tune, impersonal forces had subtly invaded. Acquiring objects and multiplying things and images within the boundaries of themselves, they had become enlarged and subtly altered. Their faces had changed.

"In the shopping malls, where people walked to worship, the multiplication of things moulded people in the image of gods. An insatiable desire for money, fame and power, an envious and obsessive need to win in the high-stakes game called life converted people into anxious human cash machines. When acquiring objects became the business of life, when the sense of self was heavily invested in objects, objects were taken in and became part of people. A monetary scale became the Judge of Life. Children were shaped in a culture of material competitiveness. Other people were productive if they had use— value. Efficiency ruled the world! It was an attitude woven from the same cloth worn by Producers and Consumers in their mutual dance.

14
Creativity and Diversity

Though all expert systems were continuously being scrapped, broken down, re-assembled, and ceaselessly changing, the Riddler had come far. The amusing but foolish little creature with an amazing brain had taken to the air and learnt to fly like the birds, travelling long distances for holidays and work. Jets shrunk the planet forever. The people made clothes from chemicals and played music by laser-beam. They strode into space and placed their feet on the moon. Satellites and space stations circled the globe. Metal-reinforced towers defied the sky. Endless tarmac tracks ran everywhere. Electronic communication became part of the experience of millions, shaping their attitudes and opinions. Computer power doubled every eighteen months.

The last years of the old century saw planet Earth wired up in a communications revolution that astounded those who lived even a generation before. Everywhere were the mobile phones and the micro-processors that outnumbered humans two to one. Online with emails and faxes, the people were now accessible anywhere, anytime. Data became a commodity that could be bought and sold: the raw material of the age. Computers started to talk to each other. Then came the birth of the Internet, the most extraordinary communication tool since prayer began. The people had never dreamt that one day they would stare at a screen to buy a house or a holiday, books, food, or an airline ticket. Every town and every person everywhere was now networked with global intelligence. The people woke up to a futuristic environment, full of robots and smart clothes. They had stumbled into a portal of computer-generated film images from digital cameras. They pinched themselves and asked whether they had been asleep for a hundred years.

And there was the challenge of gene therapy, artificial wombs, cyber sex, interactive technology, and virtual friends in a new world of nanotechnology, biotechnology, and info-technology spinning ten times faster every decade. It could transform humanity every bit as much as printing and industrial revolution. But, it also threatened to de-personalise, to offer sci-fi possibilities for exploitation on an undreamt scale, and disenfranchise those in the developing countries unable to play catch-up.

In those days, it seemed to the Peaceweaver that the whole world looked different. Even ordinary things were touched with significance and illuminated by colour. The range of human self-expression took his breath away. He was the flaneur, a stroller, walking amidst the anonymous spaces of the modern city, experiencing the complexity, disturbances, and confusions of the streets, taking in the fleeting beauty and transitory impressions of the crowds.[ii]

On every continent, he began to take in the clothing, power-dressing by pin-striped executives and eye-catching dresses worn by the glitterati of society, trousers, sarongs, jumpers, shoes of all kinds, coats for every occasion, and shirts of all colours. The range of clothing was breathtaking, reflecting the self-expression of the wearers, the image they wished to convey.

Art now became for him a witness to the riddle at

the source, the dual citizenship of humanity. On his journey, he saw the great paintings, etchings, the use of colour, idealistic images, realistic images, religious scenes, impressionism, modernism. The world was full of pictures and flashing images: the human body, scenery, pop art, advertising, portrait photography. Everything was a subject for a picture by someone who wanted to convey how they saw things. Image and reality were intertwining.

In those days, anything could be used to extract music. Music for pleasure, Easy Listening, African music, Indian music, Country and Western, background Musack in supermarkets, the great classics, spirituals, musicals—everything had to be accompanied by music. It was the most powerful communicating force in the world to stir the soul, writers and artists taking the value within their story (or lack of it) and taking it to a world outside.

Of the making of books there was still no end. Volume after volume, papers, magazines, and now online, a world of other minds was downloaded into ours. Others were gifted with drama and poetry. And so the planet filled up with theatre, films, and endless stories, enabling us to explore another life, another world. In the new world that was dawning, You-Tube as well as films and soap operas were sources of reflection and how to handle life.

The Peaceweaver saw great architecture, the art one walked into everyday. He was alive to castles, palaces, theatres, gardens, public buildings, urban boxes, and skyscrapers like manmade mountains. Medieval cathedrals and magnificent mosques transported the onlooker into a transcendent world to create a sensation of Heaven on Earth.

"And yet... and yet... the modern world witnessed anonymous, undecorated housing estates built without consultation or consideration for the wishes of their inhabitants, and with little grasp of the alienating effects of such buildings on them. Modernism had surely failed as a mass-housing and city-building project. Crime rates and continuous vandalism demonstrated that its users did not like the style or know how to decode the meaning. Was that the Protest?

All these were landscapes that the Peaceweaver observed on his journey.

THE THIRD LANDSCAPE
Deprecation

"Hath not a Jew eyes? Hath not a Jew hands, organs, dimensions, senses, affections, passions? Fed with the same food, hurt with the same weapons, subject to the same diseases, healed by the same means, warmed and cooled by the same winter and summer as a Christian is? If you prick us, do we not bleed? If you tickle us, do we not laugh? If you poison us, do we not die? And if you wrong us, shall we not revenge?" - William Shakespeare, Merchant of Venice, Act 3, Scene 1

"Guided by the belief that every life has equal value, the Bill & Melinda Gates Foundation works to reduce inequities and improve lives around the world" [iii]

"When I was in Africa, I thought that perhaps I was no less important than anyone else, though I didn't have any reason to believe this might be true" - Desmond Tutu toast on getting a BD degree, King's College London. [iv]

15
Rainbow World

"It always surprises me," said the Peaceweaver as they sat on the covered veranda watching the Asian storm. "The atmosphere is so thin. You could drive up through it in an hour. Listen to all that fighting going on right now in the lowest layer!"

Then the ferocity died away. It began to rain, the kind of rain that made no demands on anyone. A fine spray crested the eyes of his listeners and rested on their heads. Then, through the spray, the sun edged its way cautiously past the grey of overhanging clouds and lit up the evening sky. The Peaceweaver invited his guests to stand, stop, and stare.

But there was a veranda ritual to fulfil, a pre-dinner ceremony wherein guests paused to enjoy the sunset. A rainbow began to arch across the sky and then break into a multi-coloured semicircle that had no beginning and no end. The white light was split into a variety that seemed to dance as the evening sang for joy. What an act! What a drama! Its music was compulsive to anyone tuned to the welcome colours of the world.

The Peaceweaver was exhilarated that the civic leaders had responded to the concept of a community covenant, agreeing to learn together to stand up against the wretched devaluation that disfigured the world. Someone had even come up with the bright idea of encouraging people to smile at three others each day as a practical step to put the value of humans on the radar. This was a metropolitan community of many nationalities, a mixed bag of classes and teeming groups of people, diverse people that all the variations of skin colour imagination and experience could produce. Courageous conversations were taking place across the city, bringing real understanding and, in its wake, bringing people together. If his message could take off here, it could fly off any runway. So, he heard his own heart revving up as if on a race track.

"It's breathtaking," he said, "that an atmosphere can edit the sun's rays and from a palette of white light paint rainbows and twilight!

"Once," he said, "there was white light. Just white light. A monochrome reality. The white light persuaded itself that it was the only valid light, that it came directly from the central sun. It seemed to be the way things were. But, then thunder shook the world. Lightning forked in massive surges of naked electricity, a display of raw power combined with vibrating, jagged voice. After the storm clouds came the rain, and after the rain came the spray, and through the spray came the sun. And in the mysterious combination of light and sun, what the monochrome world had been concealing suddenly stood out in a colour drama to challenge perception and seek out the true nature of things. It was as if a black and white world of television and film had gained depth, magic, and colour.

"And so it was that the old Caucasian world split up. Monochrome sameness and imposing power became a scene where seven colours formed in gathering visibility. One colour was that of another class of people, the poorer masses who thronged the world but whose voice had not counted for much until their discontent became a loud Protest that could not be suppressed. Next, it could be seen that the world was divided up into two halves and that a female light dressed the sky with colours that had often been invisible.

Then came a spectrum of different colour that

before had been in the background only. Alongside was the now visible glow of those who had the advantage of years but had been sidelined. There were other colours that now stood out with unmistakable visibility. There stood out the not so subtle colour of those who had been ruled by empires from afar. And then you could see those who said they, too, were complete beings, though not endowed with all the functions seen as normal. You saw a colour of other versions of relationships that sharply challenged the monochrome world as much as anything else.

"These were not single colours carefully distinguished in the firmament. Rather, they overlapped at various points to produce a kaleidoscope. For a while, the old white male world that had been the only light over the sky had become a globe of rainbow people. The value of other colours had been rising, and in its memory, it would never revert."

While he had been speaking, on the edge of the mountains sat a globe of orange splendour, resting with a light touch and bathing the sky in rich amber glowing floods of light. Then came the dance of the purple clouds. What an act! What a drama! The guests could not stop themselves from cheering as they acknowledged that the atmosphere had put on a star performance. After a fond farewell, the sun slowly sank beneath the ridge as light departed from the summit.

A dim, diffused softness filled the Peaceweaver's voice before he regained composure, and he walked back to an empty house, silent with the intensity that clothed the small hours of the night, knowing he would look for the rainbow again.

16
The Peaceweaver's Dream: The Enchanted World

That night, he had a dream. He dreamt that, not far from there, there was an enchanted world. It was a globe suffused with glory, a place teeming with wonder, walked and stalked by amazing creatures. On this enchanted world, there were magical creatures that rode the winds and filled the skies. They swarmed, winged, and glided and sang their emancipated songs. Equipped with beaks and the feather, a marvellous device unsurpassed as an aerofoil or insulator, these flying creatures surpassed any aeronautical display that any aircraft in the world was capable of. How they navigated and flew their way home were mysteries that had the people of the enchanted world baffled. With immense variety and beauty their plumage was painted, and they had learned songs to sing. This was artistry and music at its highest, mixed with design engineering to an exact specification.

In the enchanted world, there were amazing creatures, equipped to breathe on land and under water. There were creatures called reptiles that laid eggs on land and had a special watertight skin so that they could bask in the sun and use its heat.

The wonders of that place were not limited to sea or sky. There were insect-eating mammals, winged bats that flew by sonar and plant-eaters from mice to elephants. Cows, sheep, and horses provided food, clothing, and haulage services. Hidden in the grasslands and jungles were animals with stripes, animals with long-necks, and animals that ran like the wind. Some of these creatures swung from tree to tree or were content to be ground-dwellers. But, others were hunters, combining majesty and fierce, savage power. Barking dogs and purring cats offered companionship and warmth. There were mammals equipped for cold and mammals that dwelt in the water with a heart the size of a car and a tongue the size of a hippopotamus.

But the wonders of that enchanted world had scarcely begun to unfold. There were a million tiny things that crawled and swarmed. They had highly accurate vision and navigation, an external skeleton, and a unique job description. Insects offered cleaning services, broke down organic matter, and decomposed waste back into the soil. Drawn by bright colours, they touched down from flower to flower, unknowing matchmakers of a new generation. Other forms of creatures lived in the seas of the enchanted world. They crawled on seabeds or stretched out miniscule arms to grasp some passing food. Architects of the ocean, they built intricate reefs one could see from the moon.

Swimming creatures filled the oceans, seas, and rivers with colour, variety, and food. Fish had keen smell, sharp hearing, and saw in glorious Technicolor. There were fish with vivid colouring, fish that moved with the aid of electricity, and fish that navigated to the rivers where they were hatched. And there were sharks, denizens of the deep, essential to the balance of life under the waves but condemned to swim forever.

Molluscs were everywhere, in immense variety, spreading into freshwater and onto dry land. Spiralling ammonites were the most numerous and famous of fossils in cold chilly prisons, for the enchanted planet was full of previous inhabitants of former worlds, entombed for generations in rocks.

Life on that enchanted world was a rich kaleidoscope of plants and animals, a demonstration of colour, an endless variety dwelling everywhere, a display of humour. What would it take to retrieve amazement and let it bloom into wonder?

But there was more to come. The pageant of life in that world was not only about animals. There was also the enchanted wood. It was a garden but not a carved and decorated estate; rather a garden of contrasts. Sometimes raw, rugged, wild woods; sometimes banks of softness, sometimes a blaze of colour waving gently in the wind. Someone lovingly planted the garden of flowers and left it in trust to be cultivated.

The enchanted wood was full of enormous stumps of wooden beauty, alive with sap, leaves and flower. In the scheme of things, trees would be needed to provide food and cover for wildlife and to be a source of timber, oils, perfumes, and medicines for the people of that other world. But, the forest was not just intended to be filled with towering, woody creatures of root and greenery. Flowering plants decorated the forest floor and sprung up wherever conditions bid them welcome but not just for decoration, like patterns on wallpaper. It was planned that they should provide the inhabitants of that world with shelter, clothing, medicines and food.

Imagine a place where there are only a few types of fruit or vegetables. That was not the enchanted wood. On top of all these gifts, there was a fitted green carpet that covered much of that world, brought rest to tired eyes, and broke up the barrenness.

Consciousness crept along the horizons of the sleeping man, stealthily, steadily making inroads into his drowsiness with demands that could not be ignored. At last, the day reigned. He stirred himself and then began the fight, the persistent, insistent combat he faced daily and had faced for many long months. He wearied of the struggle yet it presented itself, unbending and gladiatorial, picking a fight with him.

Suddenly, the Peaceweaver was filled with a

longing to nourish small gardens of well-being, landscapes that would weave the unpromising strands of difference and indifference into a tapestry set against the enchanted world. And he was deeply puzzled and not a little disturbed. How was it that difference in nature did not agitate people but humans were profoundly crippled by diversity amongst themselves? Why did they embrace with joyful discovery the unbounded variety of the enchanted world yet find it so hard to accept the colours and variety of the people? Why the addiction to power, superiority, and the old relegation game: so compulsive, so de-humanising.

Could they build a world where difference amongst people was no more reduced with the toxic wrapping paper of devaluation? Could the blue and white planet celebrate the range of all adorning it.

17
Then the Phone Rang...

Then the phone rang with glaring surprise. Amanda was much less brittle than usual, less clipped but somehow more urgent.

"Matt," she said after a few minutes conversation, "I've got Daniel with me."

"Daniel?" sputtered Matt in surprise. "What's he doing with you?"

"I just met him out of the blue," Amanda replied. "Look, he's in pretty bad shape and probably as angry as hell, but I've managed to persuade him to talk to you."

"Of course", Matt said, with hope surging through him. "Put him on!"

Father and son talked for a few minutes. Matthew was on the next plane home from Thailand. As the 737 cruised through the night, he sat there reflecting on the course things had taken.

Once, Daniel had been a lively, healthy boy. Despite a hidden fault line running through his life, Daniel was good at games, interested in fishing and plastic models of airplanes, of which he could boast several hundred. Matt was proud of his son. He had a sparkle.

Then the crevasse began to show. By the time he was fourteen, Daniel's circle of friends knew a local drug pusher. Daniel progressed from cigarettes to joints. His media-created icons were anxious to impress their devotees, saying that they had the answers to life and everything else. On his drug-lined road to happiness,

Daniel began to lose interest. Motivation crept away so subtly that no one knew when it went out the door. When he hit fifteen, he was withdrawn, knee deep in anxiety. By his next birthday, Daniel had moved cannabis to ecstasy. The pills of the rave culture were compelling.

"It's a dangerous, short-term bid for happiness," Matthew tried to reason with Daniel when he had confided in him one day. "You'll get chronic depression later in life. And for goodness sake, leave heroin alone. Believe me, I know what that does to you!"

But Daniel wasn't going along with common sense. He felt keenly the tedium of life. Chasing the dragon helped him cope. "You don't care how much time passes," he told his Mum.

Daniel was no longer interested in reaching his potential. Badgering from Sara merely irritated him. Relationships with his Mum and Dad broke down. Hurricanes blew up without warning. Slowly, Daniel's life disappeared in a haze of chemical happiness, as he was concerned only about the next fix and living for the present. Whenever Sara confronted him about his lifestyle or lack of any long-range goals, Daniel staunchly maintained he could stop anytime he wanted. He would just have one more fix. Like his Dad before him, he convinced himself that his behaviour was avant-garde and politically anarchic. Mat pleaded that was a distortion of history. He told Daniel that drugs and alcohol were blanking out the pain of loneliness, artificially boosting him to feel more sociable and more alive.

But Daniel didn't listened. Heroin relieved the pain just as the effect of the last dose began to wear off. He never stayed long in any of the jobs that Sara found for him. He claimed that his employers and co-worker didn't like him. Sara suspected this was just rationalisation. More likely, his needle-infested life meant that he just couldn't get to work on time.

After several years of trouble upon trouble- often with police involved, things came ti a head. One day, Daniel broke Sara's glasses, but it felt like he had trod on more than a pair from Specsavers. He had walked all over her. Matthew said he had to go. And so he went.

He met a girl. They went to Manchester. She got pregnant but didn't stay on the scene for long. Daniel still persuaded himself that things would turn out all right. When he was twenty, he met Sharon. They lived for two years in a sleazy flat with the wallpaper hanging off. Sara would never forget the day Daniel phoned in anguish to say that there was something wrong with the little girl that he and Sharon had brought into the world. It broke her heart at a time when her own body was past its sell-by-date. But after a while, Sharon left and the child was taken into care. Daniel lost his flat. He was now a dosser in Tower Hamlets One day, in a bus shelter, he bumped into Aunt Mandy. Mutual recognition flashed across the years, mutual recognition combined with nostalgic and desperate tears. Daniel had reached the end of the rope.

The next day, Matthew knocked at the door of a terrace house. The terrace was similar to all the others, an unremarkable house in an unremarkable street. The kitchen was smart; the lounge was shabby, the dining room functional. Though it was lunchtime, a pall of darkness hung visibly over the unremarkable house, as if it were a late gloomy winter's afternoon instead of a sunny autumn day. His sister answered the door. They hadn't hugged for... Well, it was a long time.

"He's in here," she said. Matt winced when he saw Daniel. A guilty expression hung over his face as if a cloud had passed over the sun. Amanda shot a sympathetic glance at him. Gone was the speech Matthew often rehearsed: "Maybe you've got to speak it out and say, 'I don't need this anymore: you're no friend of mine!' "

Daniel was well aware that heroin was no

dependable friend, or he wouldn't have ended up in that bus shelter, desperation merging into indecision, half-hoping Amanda wouldn't tell Matt. All that dissolved as the two hugged. The dam burst for both of them. "Dad," was all Daniel could manage. Then he beat his fists against Matthew with furious blows.

"It's okay," repeated Matthew over and over, holding his son but not with a one-sided sense of care being extended from one intact person to a broken jar of a young man. These were two people in pain. Sensing Matt's tears, Daniel held his Dad. Two humanities greeted and recognised each other in a painful encounter.

The next few hours were the fair-ground Matt had taken Daniel to when he was eleven. Up and down, round and round, the highs and the lows, some smiles but the anger was never far away. Volcanic simmering seemed to detect any area where the crust of emotion and reserve was wafer thin. It all came out. Matthew could only listen and try hard not to correct Daniel's narrative. That would go against the flow of his life-work and his identity, even if the emotional territory bordered on the tumour that had eaten Sara's brains.

It was a start. They had begun to dismantle the wall.

18
Addicts All

In the next town, the Peaceweaver told them of a flawed product, misshaped almost from the beginning.

"There had been no flaw in original design. The prototype was satisfactory. But, they began to go wrong. Someone threw a spanner into the works. As the factory continued to turn out its products, the flaw was now built-in. The products rolling off the assembly line seemed normal, everything in place, everything functioning, except they were flawed. Though people guessed there was something wrong, they had nothing to compare it with and knew no different. 'Presumably, this is how they make them,' they thought."

Like the arrival of a sudden thunderstorm, the Peaceweaver became indignant. The deliberate emphasis in his voice could not mask the anguish behind his words.

"Ladder makers!" he said. "We're all addicts! All of us, addicts!"

Something in his manner compelled attention and hot indignation.

"Not for us, the needle life," they said. "When did we do this," they said. "Such talk is foolish!"

His words were stinging. Words that tore, bit, and left their mark. Words that spoke of a country that had been ignored and not explored when exploring was the thing to do and not to be rejected. He spoke of a knowledge that the world had tried to drown but which arose with insistent resurrection despite every attempt to suppress it.

"You have ignored, you have rejected the truth about us. You have played games of folly and deceit, like actors taking a part in a play. 'Let's silence the voice that calls to us. We must dim our eyes so that the glimpse we had becomes but a memory.'

"I knew a sick man," he said, "oblivious to his condition yet convinced that all was well, that he had never been healthier. Yet, the flush of his illness was plain to see on his face and on his body. Though he was adamant that there was nothing wrong with him, the delusion was obvious to all. Cancer had spread with a virile embrace. If treatment had been sought, things might have been different. A few of his friends tried to reason with him. They remembered when he cut a fine figure and how he was before the glory had departed. 'You are not well,' they asserted with unceasing concern. 'See the doctor!' There would come a moment's hesitation. Then, resolute in irresolution, the sick man would waver. Denial set in once more, old instincts too strong, the old habit unbroken."

Saying this, the Peaceweaver handed round to the men and women in the market-place familiar pictures that played tricks with the mind; pictures that left them wondering: Was that a young lady or an old woman? Was that a vase or two faces?

"Can we be free to see a pattern to which our minds are blinded?" he asked.

"But, when have we seen?" they asked in consternation.

He spoke again and filled their hearts with alarm: "You have joined in a conspiracy to drown the voice of invitation and draw the curtain on what is real, you who have ladders emerging from your heads. Deny it if you can!"

"We have not engaged in conspiracy," they protested. Their protests rose and grew in clamour until it seemed a hundred voices were shouting at once. Most walked off.

But some stayed.

"Spell it out," they urged.

"We are," said the Peaceweaver solemnly, "addicted to the power of ladders." He took the step ladders he had been sitting on, erecting them against a wall. "We are built to build ladders. It is irresistible. What is this preoccupation we have with ladders? We have ladders in our heads. We are up. We are down. Yet we need to be up so that we can see others as being down. What is new, what is strange, and what challenges us must be relegated. It can never be on the same level!"

"You are crazy!" someone said.

But the Peaceweaver continued: "You have heard of the way everyone used to be somewhere on the ladder. Rich devalued the poor, landowners their peasants, and factory owners looked down on their workers. But, then we were in a different age. So, did we think the ladder had been dismantled? Addicts and devaluers all, we had to keep on playing the ladder game. Why should one half of humanity agitate the other half? Yet, from their vantage point, men looked down on inferior women. They were of lesser value.

"Those using their brains gazed down on those who worked with their hands. Head superior to hands? Language power privileged over body? In gilded superiority, white looked down on black, as if light skin had been immortalised by history. Colonial masters devalued the uncivilised in controlled paternalism. The West persisted in the assumption that it set the pace in the world. In splendid isolation, one religion devalued another, especially the conservatives amongst them, zealous to protect the interests of God."

"Old immigrants devalued new immigrants. Straights accounted gays as being of lesser worth. The fresh-faced young looked down on the grey and white haired and those gifted with supposed intactness relegated the not-so-fully-functioning to a rung marked 'disabled'. And they all devalued foreigners and confined them to going second class."

Point made, the Peaceweaver stood amongst the addicts.

"Is there any hope for our compulsive addiction?" asked the ladder makers.

The Peaceweaver listened and thought, "We yearn to find a vision we can hold on to carry us forward," he urged. "But now voices can be heard. This time we want to listen to those voices and The Voice. But can we learn a different way of seeing? To learn the truth about ourselves is the first step towards getting off the steps."

Then, with a sudden jerky movement, he kicked the ladder over. It fell with a crash.

At his invitation, though with puzzled faces, some of the audience walked up and down the flattened ladder, precariously clinging on to each other.

"Allow the pictures in our minds of others on the ladder in to jump sideways," said the Peaceweaver with hope. "Just as we know ourselves to be no longer the central sun around which all else must revolve, so we can learn the horizontal way of being! Reject the de-humanising machine that draws humans into its acid gears and crunches them into objects that can be safely relegated and conveniently placed. Ladder makers of the world! Unite to flatten your addiction!"

19
Once Upon a Time in Soweto...

Once upon a time in Soweto, everyone who was politically inclined was labelled a Communist. It was a shantytown slum in those days. Not far away, well-watered people relaxed in well-watered gardens. They were the whites. Like Liz, for instance.

Then there were those who inhabited corrugated iron shacks. They were the blacks, or the coloureds, who lived amongst dirty, dusty, unlit streets, out of sight and out of mind. When they had performed their daily service for their masters, they stepped back into the shadows of invisibility in enclaves provided. Like Leah's mother for instance.

The Peaceweaver's work as a mediator had brought him here several times before, to bring people together who wanted to knock old walls down. Facilitating this encounter was different. His sister-in-law Liz had lost her mother in the surge of violence and pain before the birth of the new South Africa. It was the last straw for the family who had emigrated to the U.K. Liz had never returned. Now she felt ready to face the past and re-connect with a privileged childhood in the suburbs of Johannesburg.

There was no one to hit out at, no one who could move out of the shadows of history with a name or a face upon whom she could pin this shattering event that still shook her from top to bottom. But, there was Leah.

South West Townships as it was once called, was a pastiche of tiny tin-roofed homes as far as the eye could see, a litter strewn landscape. In the apartheid era, the government crushed the squatter communities into a mass of shanty towns: council bungalows with two rooms, an outside toilet, and standpipe for water.

Leah greeted them in her modernised bungalow. Though not on a par with the house she had visited often, where her mother worked as a maid, she was proud of the mains drains, water on tap and electricity to power their homes. The whites had enjoyed this for years. The two women embraced. Once the distance between them was as far as the Earth to the Moon. Now they were meeting as equals, though at first Leah wanted to call Liz "Miss", as if jerked back to the time when they had played together as children. Leah quite understood the situation. Liz needed to return to allow memory and emotion to inter-weave. A part of her had died. But, now it was a time of resurrection.

They spoke for a while about the past.

"Back then, when you came to my house, when your Mum cleaned for us, I was aware of what a very different experience you would have had. We had enough, or more. They told me that black kids often scrambled amongst the refuse."

"It's true," concurred Leah with anger and sadness in her voice. "The prize was a school meal provided by the State that had been discarded by you white kids in favour of a lunch box from Mum. School meals for black and coloured children had been banned by Dr Verwoerd. If we can't feed all non-white kids, we can't feed any! That's what he said."

Leah showed Liz photos. They were of that day in June '76. The children of Soweto took to the streets in a mass protest against Bantu education and the use of Afrikaans, the language of the oppressor, as the language of instruction. Singing, they marched from school to school.

"You can't see me amongst the fifteen thousand, but I'm somewhere in the crowd," said Leah.

The police responded brutally. The world saw pictures of singing children facing attack dogs and armed police. Six hundred died. But there came a time when the humiliating self-doubt of the black population rose up with indignation and determination. "Black consciousness" they called it. Heightened self-respect by any other name.

"I can't think how we all accepted it," said Liz. "The pretence was that keeping the races apart would allow for healthy separation. But we find it enormously difficult to treat differences as equal. We have to go in for grading. Light skinned people are superior. It's how things are, or so we thought. How could I have downloaded such a programme? My primitive computer must have been wacky. To me it was so normal."

"What happened to your mother? I heard later that she died?" asked Leah softly.

Liz hesitated, and under the enquiring eyes and warmth of invitation, the river started to flow about the day when her life was sculptured with blood-stained plasticine as her father greeted her with a face such as she had never seen him wear before.

The Peaceweaver left them to it, saluting their courageous conversation. He thought about the community meeting that he was to speak at that night. Soweto was not the same as it was when Leah roamed the streets in the days of her childhood. Now there were shopping malls, cinemas, a golf course, a university and the biggest hospital in Africa— altogether, a place for the new black middle to stay rather than migrate to the old white suburbs. He wandered down the street where two Nobel Laureates had once lived. At the entrance to the Apartheid Museum were seven concrete columns, each engraved with a cornerstone of the 1994 Constitution. Democracy, equality, reconciliation, diversity, responsibility, respect, freedom: it was the most liberal constitution ever... in theory!

He went in, struck by white concrete blocks and

yellow rubble from the gold mines, past green wooden benches with the words "whites only" etched on them and the dreaded passbook. It was the instrument of humiliation blacks and coloureds had to show whenever the mood crossed a policeman's face. Liz could have gone anywhere. No place was fenced off. Beaches, parks, and toilets were free. Her family didn't have to produce the passbook except at election times to show that they could vote. Not for them the infamous pencil test: If it was inserted into you hair and remained, it showed that you had frizzy strands, and therefore, you were definitely non-white.

Words from Mandela were etched on to a granite slab: "To be free is not merely to cast off one's chains but to live in a way that respects and enhances the freedom of others."

Yes, the new South Africa had serious problems: housing, health, violence, attitudes of the new rich, economic instability, and conditions of the townships and squatter's camps — problems as high as Table Mountain. But, it had come a long way in a short time. And it was free. Or was it? Once the whites were up and the blacks were down, along with the coloureds. Now the blacks were on top and the whites were at a disadvantage in getting a job unless they had a black name. Still the coloureds were down. It made the Peaceweaver sad that the game of relegation was so addictive.

He went to re-join the two women from a fragmented past, forging a new future. But, the encounter stirred him, as all such encounters between two-way traffic should engage drivers. He spoke about it in the next town.

"The way the world was divided up has been coming to a crisis. Previous generations pursued class politics, women's rights, or black politics. A new story of equality is needed to take account of identity wars, many types of feminism and racism and the need to celebrate difference. Boundaries between accepted categories are dissolving. The very quest for emancipation conceals a protest: that we are worth more than this. This is the fundamental meaning of equality. The Protest by the depreciated is making a daring claim: 'I want to be recognised... I have the same needs... I am human, too... Treat me with respect.' "

"Don't write us off!" It was the cry he had heard of women relegated to the second division. "We're as good as you. Anything you can do, we can do. We won't be invisible any more."

"Don't write us off!" It was the cry of those of a different ethnic group consigned to the outer fringes of the circle by those who imbibed a toxic poison of racial superiority.

"Don't write us off!" It was the cry of those of a lower class or an inferior caste who had been made to travel second or even third class.

"So join this cause and campaign and covenant to learn to give value, not in principle but in practice. I will not depreciate but invest in the person whose name and face I need to look at through different eyes."

20
Half the World and Half a Man

Over the next few days, Matt and Amanda tried everywhere they could to find a drug rehab. Eventually, they found a suitable hostel, where the programme would give Daniel sufficient structure to re-route his addictive life. Matt was deeply moved that Mandy was reaching out to help Daniel. It was a turning point.

They sat on Saturday having a bite to eat. A weathered, auburn-haired woman was approaching, clutching a tray as she picked her way through a crowded restaurant. While chatting to Daniel, Matt shot a glance at Mandy.

"How's life treating you?" was all that Matt could muster, though it struck him as being trifling and fumbling, utterly incapable to do justice to the encounter. For a few moments, they ate their meal in silence. It was her eyes that were the most striking part of her persona, eyes that were caverns of mystery. What lay in those depths? Playfulness or vulnerable pain? Reserve or invitation?

They sat for a while in silence. The deep fried pepperoni visibly shrank. Though she would never have admitted it, Mandy was an emotionally needy person with a huge appetite for love that was obscured by her natural reserve and an aura of coldness. There seemed no access, no route in. She was a personality in disguise.

"Can we ever understand what goes on in our own heads?" she wondered as they tucked into the pepperoni. Her brows knotted as she struggled for expression.

Conversation ranged briefly across continents, time zones, and families. Then it went deeper. They were both swimmers arising from the murky depths to re-surface.

"Am I allowed to ask if you have a boyfriend or are you still the ardent feminist?" Mat asked.

"Yes to both!" answered Amanda. "For centuries, Western society has been unsure about how to treat women. Are we Mary or Eve?" she added smiling. "They have the right to work wherever they want to, as long as they have dinner ready when you get home. That's John Wayne," said Amanda, her smile broadening even further.

"Ah yes. Shintaro Ishihara, the controversial Tokyo mayor caused outrage in Japan when he said it was pointless for women to go on living after menopause," remarked Matthew, observing the ritual. "Jack was a misogynist, though," he added, observing Amanda's reactions. She merely averted her gaze and carried on.

"Despite, or maybe because of home, I was part of the new world. We weren't going to be edited out of the script. I was too young to fight the equal pay for equal work battles but adamant that we were going to re-shape the world with feminine norms!

"Like you, I had my time in industry, though I didn't much enjoy the glass ceiling or being harassed and humiliated by my boss. The company response to a male who was abrasive, rude, and confrontational was to accept these features as positive and to do nothing about them. In a female, they were seen as wholly negative. At least teaching is a job where equality has been a part of the deal," she added.

By now, the pepperoni was shrinking fast. Amanda chose not to tell her brother about Jim Fleming. Invariably, when it was over, she would lie with her back to him. Jim's wife, Susan, was the one whom he went back to on weekends or late at night. It was always going to be like this. Why had she let him in? Her thoughts went back to the staff Christmas outing when she had felt her biological clock ticking. "Maybe I should have a child while I still can," she had reasoned. "But not him!"

Too late. The coastal defences of reserve eroded, and she realised that she was swimming in a direction fatal to caution, snared, as much as any addict is snared, with a substance she needed.

"I would describe myself as a post-feminist now," Amanda said, re-grouping herself.

"I try to listen to the music. What background theme do you reckon is playing there?" asked Matthew.

"Meaning women aren't prepared to see themselves as victims. We celebrate diversity rather than go for equality, being ourselves for God's sake. Why would we girls want to be like a jumped-up, stupid bloke?"

Amanda frowned and then continued. "The battle is not over. In the West, with a few exceptions, women no longer go second class. Women aren't prepared to be second class or cheap labour. Some parents of my pupils have a lot to contend with, mind you," Amanda said. "I think of one family trapped in a hovel of a house where the Mum is deaf, plus she is Bangladeshi. That scores points for social exclusion on anybody's register. It's only in theory that she can become a doctor, manager or Prime minister!"

Matthew felt the protester in him catch fire. Amanda paused to pour herself a drink. Then she went on with the air of a practised debater whom one would hope was on his side.

"The struggles we face here, though, are on a very different level to what women in the poorer world have to endure. Women are completely subservient and inferior to men. Their place is defined by stifling tradition and religion. They work long hours in the fields in back-breaking labour. A hundred years to change? It's all too slow."

"I've seen some of that on my travels. It all resonates with a talk I'm giving soon," observed Matthew.

"How is your work going?" Amanda asked.

"Hard to say, because I don't know any way of judging real success," responded Matthew, a seeming evasiveness concealing nonplussed confusion.

"There is a real movement for change out there. People realise, I think, that the old ways have led to conflict and yet more conflict that only sucks the life out of things. Yet," he added, "like all campaigners before or since and anyone involved with these new social movements, I suppose it's hard to give shape to the message in a way that people can get hold of and get behind. I have hundreds of hits on the web-site from all over the world, so that is a green shoot. And of course there are plenty of us working in this area, including you, of course. For too long, we have said we can recognise the value of humans but not value half the world. It won't wash anymore.

"I have travelled in Iran" he added with passion. "Whatever one thinks about the Chador, a woman is only worth fifty percent."

"Am I right in thinking that any evidence she gives in court counts for half of a man's?" asked Amanda.

"Yes," agreed Matthew. "Compensation for injury or death is only fifty percent of what a man gets. Many women are no longer willing to be repressed. There is a Campaign for Equality under way, but it's highly dangerous. Get involved and risk serious intimidation. Keep a bag packed!"

"I'd like to get on board with your work," said Amanda. "Behind different causes, it's common ground. Email me the notes of your talk."

Coffee arrived, courtesy of the auburn-haired waitress. So did the bill. Amanda paused to check it, insisting on paying. Reaching out to Daniel, Amanda was brilliant. It was a real opening in both directions. The wall was definitely coming down in Tower Hamlets.

21
How the Other Half Lives

As the Peaceweaver continued his journey, he took up a lament for the violence that was perpetrated on the female spirit and the female body.

The experience or threat of violence affected the lives of women everywhere, cutting across boundaries of wealth, race, and culture. In home and community, in times of war and peace, women were beaten, raped, mutilated, and killed with impunity. The World Health Organisation had estimated that one woman in five would be a victim of rape or attempted rape in her lifetime. Rape was a weapon of war as Yugoslavia disintegrated. The deadly virus in men's minds broke again in Darfur.

Pornography reduced women to the level of objects and things. Women did not exist as humans but were merely there to satisfy a man's desire.

In the civilised West, one woman in four experienced violence at home. Many studies in different countries said that maybe two out of five women experienced domestic violence. It was a major cause of death and disability for a woman between the ages of sixteen and forty-four as she embarked upon a career of being a woman and a mother. In the United States, land of the free, a woman was raped every six minutes. Every fifteen seconds, a woman was battered.

The spectre of domestic violence involved deadly magic that transformed a person into an object, an object who was then ripe for battering. In traditional societies, husbands could do what they wanted with their wives. It was merely a different recipe for the domestic violence brewing elsewhere. In a globalised world, the trafficking of women became a worldwide phenomenon in which victims were sexually exploited, forced into labour, and subjected to abuse. Murders of women in Guatemala, Russia, India, and Pakistan often went un-investigated and unpunished. In Pakistan most rapists and killers went free because of poor policing and the victim's fear of speaking out. Gang rape and honour killings of women remained common in a country where feudal and tribal systems still too often held sway.

Across Asia, a woman was worth only half a man. When it came to marriage, divorce, and custody of children, the world was in charge of the other half of humanity. Forced marriages still pressed many women into unwelcome relationships. They were at the mercy of a bridegroom, who could quickly become tired of them or feel aggrieved at the lack of dowry. Then they turned violent. In India, the dowry system could lead to tragic results. Every year, six thousand brides were murdered by their husbands, furious that they had received no money. In China, government birth-control policies restricted families to a single child. So thirty millions girls were missing. Female circumcision, a traditional custom in many African countries sought to ensure that women should restrict sexual pleasure. Each year, more than two million girls in thirty countries had to undergo this mutilation, because the community prized chastity in a girl until she married. The alternative was no husband and no economic security.

From infancy, girls in many lands received less food, less medical care, and less education than their brothers. Each year, thousands of women and girls were trafficked into forced prostitution.

Prejudice against girls started early. The life cycle of violence started with sex-selective abortion and infanticide in countries where girls are valued less than boys or considered an economic burden. Boys were future breadwinners who will look after parents in old age. Girls were a financial burden.

What could he say? What was there to say?

THE FOURTH LANSCAPE
Desecration

"The more physical, emotional and verbal abuse he received, the more he expected it, eventually believing what they were telling him that he was useless and worthless and stupid, a fear he keeps in a dark place".[v]

"A person is a person because of other people" - African Proverb

"Dawn will come and the girls will ask about her, 'Where is she?' And the monster will answer: 'We killed her.' A mark of shame was on our foreheads, and we washed it off" - a female Iraqi perspective on honour crimes. [vi]

22
Verbal Daggers and the Unchosen Community

She wore a far away expression. Scenes of her life flashed before her. She felt that she had lived half a lifetime amidst a tribe of people with an empty, shallow existence, a tribe of which she was a prominent member. Once, Liz dwelt in a green world bathed by golden sunshine. In the unquiet moments of tossing night, she would hear Mum and Dad call to her as they always used to. Her mother was warm, busy, church-going. Her Dad was a lawyer who loved Liz but disguised it heavily amidst a strict regime. As a girl, she could always be found by the river near their home. Then Mum passed away and death dried up the river.

"What happened to your mother?" asked the Peaceweaver gently.

Liz remembered the phone call announcing an act of random violence, a single gun-shot on a crowded Johannesburg street. Out it all came: the gunshot aimed at someone else, her mother experiencing the disintegration of tissue and muscle and blood, and then nothing. "This can't be true," she and her Dad said a hundred times. Why were limbs normally so finely tuned, strangely numb, as if a victim of a stroke, not grief? Liz's Mum was pronounced dead at the scene by a police surgeon. Later they had to go to the police station. They said a post-mortem was being carried out. The funeral could be held in a couple of days. It was some white man responsible.

Her father attended to it all with mechanical

efficiency, hearing his own voice as a stranger announcing startling news to the uncomprehending. For two hours that evening, they sat in their lounge, trying to get involved in an old film. There was nothing to say. What was there to say? Half way through the night, Liz disappeared into the kitchen to rustle up a snack. Her father was up. Sleep was impossible. They sat in the dining room, eyes meeting. Did the wretched guy who fired the wretched shot have any clue as to the thousand metre wave of grief that engulfed them, wave after furious wave of wretched grief from a wretched shot from some wretched guy on a wretched street.

She had some inkling of the routine violence Leah's mother had lived with. "Where have you been, Dorcas?" they would ask. And they would hear there had been another stabbing in the family or of a neighbour.

Now Liz shuddered at the memory, still exacting tribute. She needed to change the subject, so she tacked, like a yacht bending before the wind.

"Tell me," she asked, "why can't Steve and I just talk?" she wondered in disbelief. "If, as you say, we are born for connection, what ultimate mysteries lie behind the many misunderstandings that dog our lives? If sharing thoughts and feelings is the royal road to the depth we were born for, why do we dig so long and hard to find it?"

Steve knew how to control his anger, but real intimacy was a stranger in that household. Words were for throwing, not healing, sharp knives with jagged edges.

The Peaceweaver stirred. A great sadness crept upon him stealthily.

"But how true this is," he said after a while, "to interaction between all people, to parents with their children, to people with neighbours, to diverse races and nations. We must penetrate the mystery of a different soul that enriches us, the otherness of another. Learning to communicate makes or breaks the tattered spirit. If we are committed to depth, we must take the road necessary to find it, though we learn a different language."

He remembered how, even after his step-father's funeral, when they had got home, a misunderstanding between his brother and Liz boiled over. Within a short space of time, they had forgotten what the trigger was that started the guns firing. Steve evidently thought Liz was getting at him again, as he put it, underlining the word "again" forcefully. At first, Liz was sullen. Then they went for it with hammer and nails, scoring points that left each other angry, resentful, without winners. Liz later stood in her kitchen, alone, bruised, triumphantly wearing a confused look that questioned if any triumph was worth it. Guns, hammer and nails, knives— all were deployed.

"You must think we're always like this," she said. "We're not really. But we do have no-go areas. If I press in on Steve's tender spots, woe betide me. Why all the rows?"

"Ah the rows!" said the Peaceweaver after a few minutes of empathic unsettling had done their work. Steve and Liz seemed to have such inability to settle disputes of everyday life by peaceful means. The vocabulary and process was just not there. The slightest tension quickly escalated into thermonuclear warfare, either that or sullen, silent withdrawal: a cold war that went on for days with little ground between.

"You have been thrown together in the unchosen community of the family," he reflected after a while. "A special place where gift and education meet, the family was designed to bring a gift of shelter that protects and nurtures. And it was to be a bearer of the gift of identity, a setting that locates and defines us. In one family we are born, the other we formed. We are somebody's children; we are somebody's parent. Here was a school for living, a sheltered place of education. Here we were to learn about role models, about conflict and how to resolve it, about feelings and how to express them, about relationships and how they work, about trust, how that can be built but so easily destroyed. This education was to initiate us into the boundaries between genders and generations. Above all, we were meant to learn the skills to build relationships and sustain the depth that is an echo of another world. But here, too, we learn the skills of unarmed verbal combat!"

Liz nodded in agreement.

"It is vital to allow another a right to their story," observed the Peaceweaver. "To deny someone his narrative is to shut him down in an act of avoidance, without which bullying does not survive. Instead of being healing and soothing places, for many relationships are war zones where destructive forces rage violently."

Liz said that she would try to cross the emotional Gulf Stream that separated her from Steve, to try to see the world through his window. Would that evoke reciprocation? The Peaceweaver could not say. It was worth a try.

23
The Song of the Hunter and the Hunted

But, the conversation plunged him into deep thought. One day came a moment of insight, as if signs in a foreign country had suddenly changed to one's mother tongue. Those who were devalued moved across human landscapes in which they too were devaluers. Those who were oppressed could become expert oppressors in another drama. Dividing up the world between oppressors and oppressed was naive.

But people were conditioned to driving up a one-way street. They could not take in that people were capable of inflicting hurt and driving dangerously out of choice. Or they could not ascribe fault to their own side. It was a blind spot that affected drivers the world over.

"On, my journey," he said to the people, "I have seen that we are both hunters and the hunted. We cannot fathom life unless we understand that a broken world is both what we do to others and what they have done to us. Both insights are needed without which we only see in part." The song of the hunter and the hunted gave him a more complete vision, a song he had come to hear amidst the music of the world.

Deep in the heart of the world, something had been broken. Steadily, it was borne upon the Peaceweaver that there was a fundamental distortion at the very centre of things. More than a piece missing, there was a warp drive taking the occupants in wrong directions, always pushing boundaries where no man had gone before. The effects could be seen everywhere, but the cause lay hidden.

"And the cause?" they asked him.

"The cause," said the Peaceweaver, "is conversion, the conversion of humans into objects. Objects that are devoid of colour, feelings, rational motivations such as ours or the soaring gift of imagination; objects that can be misplaced and defaced- card-board cut-outs whose story is unimportant."

He told the people of an ancient play that had stood the test of time and was still doing the rounds. Despite the original script not being followed, the actors went on, oblivious and unaware. Generation after generation, the drama had been acted out, in every society and on every continent. Every village, town and city had its own version, coloured with local flavour and costumed with the clothing of the day. But, the actors rarely looked at one another to ask, "Is this supposed to be in the script? Should we be saying this?"

On his journey, violence weighed heavily upon a world where it was dressed up as a solution or portrayed as normal. He heard everywhere strident notes of violence and destruction, laws trampled on, relationships shattered. It was a deeply disturbing sound, the sound of greed and pride, the sound of selfishness, of men marching to war, a depressing litany of broken people and broken dreams in a broken world. If it wasn't the clenched fist, it was the boot. If it wasn't the boot, it was the knife. If it wasn't the knife, it was the gun. If not the gun, it was the bomb.

Five ways to assault; five ways to assert. A knife was designed to puncture. Firing a bullet from a metal rod that was an extension of the person: a bullet designed to rudely penetrate the complicated formation of tissue, brains, and blood. A bomb was designed to dissolve; dissolve a human. But a clenched fist was also a hand, a hand at the end of an arm put around the distressed, the hand of friendship to the friendless. And putting the boot in was also a foot that could run to someone's aid.

24
The Market Place

The Peaceweaver brought his message to a close. Before him the sea of faces was crested with a fine spray of eyes that once were dead but now were alive again. He stood in the public square framed by houses and shops. Behind him, a market bustled. Canvas frames flapped in the wind. The Peaceweaver spoke once more.

"Come in," said the Peaceweaver. "Walk right in, all who feel keenly the desolation of the wasteland that the desecrating violence has created. Calling all those who feel the bankruptcy of our civilisation, wondering where to look for inspiration! Come on in and browse. Take your time. No longer will we be told what to believe or what to buy. An unparalleled range of foods is now yours, a vast choice of clothing or leisure pursuits. We stand at the centre of our own world, able to select the items, food and people we want. Our shelves are never empty. Take something away and there will be alternatives. Here in this supermarket, what is right for us is a personal choice. All lifestyles are on offer for all have the same price tag."

But was there not a fatal flaw in that very boldness? Everything was on offer, nothing was on offer. Still the canvas flapped in the wind. But, something else was brewing. A fight was breaking out. His audience looked on, nonplussed as shoppers fought with traders in a rude scuffle. Then they stopped to look at the Peaceweaver. He was offering mirrors to the passers-by, cheap at the price.

"Why do you call us to reflect on our violence in

this market place?" they asked him.

"It is not just a place of acquisition; I show you a place of exchange," said the Peaceweaver. "Here people bring goods that are soiled, defaced, and marred in many an angry scene. Because of the violent encounters, the goods have lost value."

It was true. Wanting a refund, people were bringing items back that were disfigured and broken. And they were trying to exchange these goods for new, the incomplete for the complete, the broken for the whole. Needless to say, the offers were rejected, requests denied. Then the on-lookers recoiled in horror. Someone was clawing at the face of a seller, trying to get his money back or replace what had been lost.

"What is your point?" they asked him after a while.

The Peaceweaver grew sad.

"Where there is a gap, they will fill it. Where there is erosion of value because of the violence, they must make up the loss. It cannot be that there is loss. Complete the full measure we must; compensate we must. We have no choice, for we are made to have a full measure. And we will take and scrape the loss off the face of another being to make up the unsettling deficiency."

Most of the crowd passed on at this point. Some understood that he was trying to help them see the violence of the world through a different lens. What would that mean to glimpse the exchange that goes on in the emotional transactions that shaped that violence? Your value for mine if I have to; my grievance, my offence, my hurt needing compensating for, forcibly if I have to; your face for my loss of face; your respect to cover the nakedness of my disrespect. The lashed became the lashers; those who lived with brokeness became the breakers; the hunted became the hunters, and the resentful provoked resentment.

"There is that within that pursues its value," said the Peaceweaver. "And we will not rest until we find it. The question is how and where and why."

25
Clare and the Art of Peaceweaving

Not many signed on that day to stand against the desecration within and around them. So, he spoke to them once more.

"For all who wish to stand against the politics of recycling, an eye for an eye, who will buy one of my puppets?"

From the folds of a beautifully ornate suitcase, he drew a girl puppet. It was a suitcase such as could only have come from the bazaars of Kashmir, but the puppet was from everywhere. And though dusk was preparing to settle over the market place, there was sufficient clarity to see the puppet attempting to ride what looked like a bicycle. After a few attempts, the girl puppet succeeded. Then something happened. Bestriding the cycle, she fell deliberately. In the Peaceweaver's hands, the cycle crashed. Great was its fall. It lay on the ground with a wheel lying beside. The puppet looked sheepishly triumphant.

"Her name is Clare. It speaks to us of a way of breaking the repetition," he said.

"Spell it out," the passers-by said.

"There are five steps," replied the raconteur.

"Create a space to be heard; that is the first step we must take. For want of a space to allow the voices to be heard and the stories told, those voices will become violent exchanges. Create places and multiply opportunities for deliberate exposure to the dissonant sound of another without which the language of the unheard will reign."

"And the second step?" they asked him.

"*L*isten to the music!" he urged them. "Listen to the music, for without it we will never change the song between us. Tune in, tune in to the themes playing in the background of your opponent's song, to the concerns and fears you cannot discern so readily playing subtly behind the chords that come to you with obvious insistence. Do not be afraid to sing your own song but adjust to the underlying notes supporting the melody. Without such hearing, we shall never find harmony".

"What of the third step?" they enquired.

"*A*llow someone else a right to their song, for the essence of control is denial of a narrative. It is when allowance of another's window on their world is mutually given that the voices can resonate and songs of protest can be heard without being shut down."

"And what of the fourth step?" they asked him.

"*R*ecognise the worth of another," he urged them. "Once the space has been cleared and the songs can be discerned, once it is allowed that someone else may sing his song, there can be sight given to all that each pursues his value in the marketplace of the world and that each is compelled to Protest its erosion. Recognise that others have a value, too, similar to your own. That will be the royal road to forgiveness, for when it is breached, a transaction has taken place that calls out for recompense".

"And the fifth step to breaking the cycle?"

"*E*ngage with singers of other songs. Engage in reconciling acts. Trade in the marketplace without scraping value off the face of another trader. So those acts will be acts of vision and of courage, acts that re-image the torrid landscapes of this world, acts that create harmony, acts that weave peace from the unpromising materials of difference and indifference. In this way, all will win."

"We will buy your puppet" they said, "for that is a world we seek: a world that weaves that which is inside us and that which lies outside."

He sold lots that day. It was the most hopeful sign for a long time.

26
A Strange Tale of Domination

"What have we done to the world?" he wondered. Every day the lament grew louder.

On his journey, he had seen vast stretches of Mediterranean coast concreted over. The ugliness and the noise were keeping visitors away. As mass tourism was about to take off in the developing world, development threatened to destroy the very things people wanted to enjoy.

In China, "Man must conquer nature!" had summed up the Great Leap Forward. But ten percent of the forests had been felled. Later, the Communist Party said that to live in harmony with nature was part of social harmony. It seemed a throwback to a much older time yet the world over; people sought a harmonious balance with nature.

The wandering armies of the poor haunted him. Reluctant migrants and asylum seekers were on the move, surging into fortunate nations. He saw the spectre of famine— a third of the world starving and a third of the world under— fed while the rest were busy dieting. At the dawn of the millennium, over six billion people now stood on planet Earth. The last billion had been added in eleven years. Now there were eighty million new mouths to feed every year in a world running out of land. People had stained the oceans, a life support system for the planet. They destroyed coral reefs, rain forests of the sea. Food chains were slipping down into a marine junkyard dominated by plankton. Rivers and streams were disgorged with effluent from manufacturing plants and untreated sewage. Rivers and lakes were dead. The water was sick. How could water be both the bringer of life and of death?

Amidst wonder, there were many ominous, darker signs that littered the blue and white world. On his journey, some roads had only occasionally been interrupted by meadows. Out of town shopping centres, petrol stations and restaurants sprouted everywhere, occupying territory that once infiltrated was lost forever.

People were haunted by the ghosts of living things lost and gone forever. Country after country had sawn through their inheritance. Countless species of animals had been sacrificed for land and illegal trade. The birds were flying into extinction. Thousands of species were becoming but a memory or photograph, a reminder of an enchanted world that begged to be re-introduced to the inhabitants of the blue and white world.

The same strategy of devaluation and domination that had distorted relationships between ethnic groups, between genders or classes had disfigured the natural world.

People had done violence to nature, as if it were a separate realm. "Yours to exploit!" Maybe, thought the Peaceweaver, extending value to fellow humans was woven from the same cloth as valuing the Earth, which was part of people and people a part of it. If you respected someone, you would not foul or litter their garden.

Unless people learned to value more than just themselves, it was clear that they stood to lose even that. And so he taught the people to listen to a theme playing in the background, a harmony with the world to which much violence had been done. With the value of the people, this emphasis seemed to him to be a conjoined twin.

27
The Darkest Hour of the Night

Amanda kept glancing at the phone anxiously, hoping it would ring just for her and a familiar voice would caress her with softly spoken intimacy. Jim had said he would call. But, the phone observed a Sabbath. Her text messages bounced back with insouciance. Then her phone buzzed. It was her nephew Daniel. He was in trouble.

He had been chased along the street, along with a friend of his. Daniel had been stabbed and was lucky to escape with his life. His friend was not. The men had run off laughing. A passer-by had tried to stem Daniel's bleeding with a towel in the communal doorway of her block of flats.

So there sat Amanda in the casualty area of the hospital, looking around her, waiting for Daniel to be seen. The tea towel was still wrapped round his arm. It was 2.45 in the morning. One man sat with his head in his lap, holding a towel to his eyes.

"It was meant to make you mad!" erupted a loud voice in the corner.

Clearly a fight had developed outside a nightclub. The bouncer had intervened and, in the scuffle, had pushed them through a shop window. Across hospitalised rows of red seats, both parties now glared at each other. In its way, it struck Amanda as a little picture of Hell, an advanced warning of a day of reckoning.

"What a mess"s he thought. "People messing up and lashing out. They're trapped," she thought. "Trapped!

Trapped!"

And why had the bleeding returned?

The door opened. It was Matt. They hugged and chatted for a while, watching hurt people meander through the reception area. Occasionally, a nurse walked briskly through from one end to another, walking faster than most can run. In the middle of the night, everyone and everything was daubed with grim colours. The sign on the wall was unmistakable: "This hospital will not tolerate abuse or assaults on its staff!"

"They reckon it was the drug people who stabbed him," Matthew said. "Daniel owed them £3,000. He was very lucky. The knife evidently missed the main target".

Amanda whistled under her breath. "All this waiting round in hospitals must bring it all back with Sara?" she said, fishing.

"I can never forget it," agreed Matt with saddened face. "It's been two years now."

Just then, Daniel went to make a statement. Matthew sat looking at the tear stained lives and anger that had sicked up all over the place. The record in Casualty that night stirred him deeply. "We definitely pay," he thought, "just like someone's going to pay for that shop window." He ached for Daniel, emerging from his small cold prison only to be stabbed that evening by the drug people. He was lucky to be alive.

"During the last two months," said Amanda suddenly, "I've been having a strange dream. It's of our house in Malmesbury when we were kids. It keeps recurring."

"Tell me?" Matt enquired.

"Okay, but don't laugh. I dream that we have rooms in our house we didn't know were there. It's like... it's like there's a landing or a suite of rooms that were there all the time but remain unoccupied. The access is through a separate door, a door that I glimpse sometimes but never go through. It's one of these old wooden doors with vertical panels. One day, I'll go through and find out what lies on the other side."

Suddenly, Matt was reminded of those pictures on the wall in Daniel's room, pictures that helped his son explore dark visions. Sara would dust in his bedroom once a week and look up, wondering if there were any new additions. At first, she hardly noticed them. Then she saw first one, then two pictures, scenes framed in dark colours of a boy fighting off bad men and ghosts, of demons that appeared to be walking with arms outstretched towards a boy whom she took to be Daniel. The year before her diagnosis, the pictures changed to more hopeful images of sunrises and bright lights.

Daniel was in Casualty for ages, being stitched up after the knife had cut him and interviewed by the police. Matt and Amanda dozed as much as a hard chair in Casualty would allow. It was a long time since she had heard from Jim. She thought of the child growing inside her. The child would be safe, never raised in a world of sandpapered edges or having to endure what she had, whatever it was that disturbed her.

But the next day, with Daniel discharged, the bleeding returned, a thin red line that continued to haunt her. Why was her own body doing this to her? Didn't it know she wanted this child? She wanted to scream at her own body, as if it were blindly following a programme that must be halted immediately. But, the doctor was grim.

"I'm afraid that, unless the bleeding stabilises, the prognosis is not good".

"Not good?" she repeated in disbelief.

Two days of bed rest followed. On the third day, the bleeding returned strongly, and they confirmed the miscarriage. Amanda had a DNC and was then allowed to go home.

Matthew was there, waiting for her with a bunch of

roses. They embraced, but no tears flowed. "Even in distress, she's dignified," he thought. Then she wept quietly, accepting, without words, the tissues he extracted from the box in her kitchen. After a few moments, Amanda regained a semblance of composure.

"The baby's gone," she said without emotion.

He left after a while, shutting the door on a woman whose inner being was disintegrating.

"I'm being punished," thought the lady on the demolition site. "I wanted to cheat him."

She tried to place a call on his mobile to tell him. Then Amanda dissolved into tears, weeping for the child that would never know life. Her grief would have been painful to witness if there were any witnesses.

Throughout that long night, images kept blurring together like slide projector images on the wall of her memory. Flashes dimly formed but were gone, hauntingly, before she could get a fix. As she struggled to sleep, she remembered long ago nights of elusive sleep, when she was too terrified to close her eyes.

Recurring nightmares began to form a pattern. There were hands over her face and then her body, a dark shadow of a stranger whose face she fought to recognise. Amanda sat up panting heavily, her stomach knotted as the dark images leered out of the shadows and stood to attention.

It was her stepfather! Dark secrets in a darkened room arose from under the sheets, skeletons shaking her chains in her face, mocking her. Blanked out horrors of what Jack did when they were alone rose up from nowhere. Amanda watched as a spectator, watching with fascinated objectivity, watching in slow motion forgotten memories of being a wife substitute for her step-father who came to her most nights.

What was this? What on Earth was going on? She dimly realised that the miscarriage must have triggered memories long suppressed. One child dying who had lived. Another child coming back to life who had long since been dead. Coming back to life on the third day. Dark secrets in a darkened room. Amanda couldn't remember crying before she was twelve. In fact, a full year of her life had been ripped from her memory. So, it was amnesia then, the amnesia that stopped people from going insane! She had entered the other room. Would it be a room of named terror or an ante-chamber to a wider hall of liberation? But for three days, shaking was the order of things.

    She knew she had to tell Matthew what she had seen. He would understand why she had been brittle and distant, that she blamed him and Steve for Dad's death that had led them all to life with Jack, who would visit her in the darkest hour of the night. He would understand that she didn't now need to be forever trapped in her story, forever bound by the life-compelling narrative.

28
The Cry of the Children

Somewhere in history, a child was crying. It was not the tears of a baby exercising its lungs or of a little boy or girl hurt from falling over and gashing a leg. It was a young life torn apart, mutilated, ripped in two, burnt and disfigured for life.

It was one amongst a million and a half victims of administrative mass murder of children, routine policy, "chasing the children up the chimney" in the gas ovens. The child crying was an orphan, a horrified spectator of war, when it's father and mother were killed before him on the day the soldiers came, orphaned again and again when that terrible day was revisited and recalled.

Or a child of the past, not perfect in shape, who cried too much or cried too little. What terrifying indictment of humanity when uncomprehending infants were thrown into rivers, flung into dung-heaps or cesspits, placed in jars to starve to death or exposed on hillsides as food for animals. Until the day before yesterday, disposable children were an accepted, everyday occurrence.

The cry of the children was century after century of battered people growing up to batter their own children, whole epochs where discipline was savage and the time parents gave to their children was a minimal gift, quickly withheld.

The cry of the children was from a million, even in

a country like the U.K., who had experienced neglect, maltreatment, or the ugly face of abuse, where 100,000 children ran away from home every year.

The cry of the children was from a boy or a girl who would draw forever upon a legacy of life-long haunting. The cry of the children was from Chinese women who remembered the day their foot-binding began. Reducing the size of a women's feet created an unnatural hobbling that aroused men. It was for institutional cruelty that generation after generation of girls were praised for putting up with extreme pain of broken bones for life, women and their families together devoted to a cruel eroticism.

The world still destroyed the lives of its children. Over half the world was now a vulnerable child.

The Peaceweaver saw the global menace of child prostitution, ten million innocent lives deflowered in sex tourism, a million children in South-East Asia traded each year, a million and a half children forever contaminated by HIV. He grieved over the millions aborted in the West over thirty years. He was haunted by the pied-piper song of a chemical induced route to happiness amongst teenagers. It was the cry of the children. The cry of the children arose from a paedophile ring, with its covertly advertised Internet activities. He shouted at such electronic prostitution, taking the sin in men's minds and projecting it like some instant virus spreading muck across the world.

What had happened to the children? Were people deaf to their cry?

If it didn't destroy its children, it demonised them. Children, even in the West, were feral creatures, insensitive and cruel, especially to be feared in packs.

The cry of the children came from a boy who had trod on a landmine. There was a stump where his foot used to be. The cry of the children was from one of a 150,000,000 orphaned street kids, glad to find any scrap of warmth in the sewers in winter or food from dog-scavenged rubbish or twice that number chained up in enslaved child labour.

The cry of the children was the ten million children under five who died in one year from disease or lack of food. And the next. And the one after that.

It was the cry of spoilt, trampled childhood and lost innocence from teenagers strutting around with Kalashnikovs, where the gun was the medium of exchange. It was the child soldiers who haunted Africa, joining civil wars that were blighting a continent, forced to join guerrilla armies and be transformed into killing machines.

"Weep," he said, "for the two million children who were victims of war or the four million disabled by war over the previous decade. Hear the cry of the kids targeted in the Rwandan genocide, whose massacre was ignited by an inflammatory radio broadcast. 'To kill big rats, you have to kill the little rats.'"

The child crying was among the boys of Bethlehem put to sword in the jealous rage of a king who feared a rival would eclipse him. "A voice is heard in Ramah, of weeping and great mourning, Rachel weeping for her children, refusing to be comforted because they are no more."

THE FIFTH LANDSCAPE
Dehumanisation

"I was not permitted to see my mother or father or poor sisters and brothers to say goodbye, though going to a strange land and might never see them again. The people who keep slaves think black people are like cattle, without natural affection. But my heart tells me it is far otherwise."
- Mary Prince, 1831 [vii]

"My instructors told me that this is how I can serve God, by attacking Britain and American." - a young British Jihadist in Afghanistan. [viii]

"The frivolity of it all. We are like mischievous apes tearing up the image of God." [ix]

29
An Algerian Evening

It was a night when diamonds lay sparkling on the waters. The modern part of the city was built on the level ground by the seashore. The French called it Alger la Blanche for the glistening white of its buildings rising up from the sea, but they were being shrouded with shadows. Flower sellers plied hotel guests as they sat drinking on the terrace, touched by a warm breeze that caressed and played with them. In every direction, thirty-foot high matted date palms spread across the grounds. The moon climbed out of the sea with an orange glow that, at first, barely tipped the gathering night and then slowly rose into an Algerian evening.

For a while, the Peaceweaver watched, fascinated, as the moon climbed higher, assuming a brilliance and a sharpness that brought its craters within reach of his hands.

After he had spoken, the Peaceweaver continued a conversation with a group of listeners. Their talk was of the world and how beauty and misery could be woven together in such a fabric. And in the thread of their conversations, it was clear that life had to be woven from unpromising materials of difference and indifference.

Their attention on the hotel veranda was interrupted by the sound of laughter coming from the bar behind. It seemed to be the rustling sound of people pursuing close relationships, picking their way through the maze of constant encounters, demonstrating soft, warm createdness, playing out what it was to be intensely human: the highs and the lows, the triumph and the despair. As the evening wore on and they ate and drank in the stillness of the night, they admired the peacefulness of that scene and how darkness temporarily threw a blanket over the surrounding hills. Soon only the outline was visible. They talked of their travels. Mountain peaks, rivers, lakes, waterfalls, deserts— how much the landscapes of Earth had shaped the stage scenery, the setting against which the drama of human life had been played. They looked up, wondering what it would be like looking down. A breeze began to direct gentle coolness upon them.

"Smells and waste would overwhelm us were it not for the refreshing wind," he said. "If it were divided among the people of the world for an inheritance, the legacy would last each of us a thousand lifetimes. The envelope of air is addressed to us but rarely acknowledged. Imagine a world without wind. How dry and airless it would be, a world without moisture, no soil, no life."

Tranquillity was belied by reality. It was hard to believe that not far away, not long before, a car bomb detonated in the Ben Aknoun district, near the Supreme Constitutional Court. Ten minutes later, in the Hydra neighbourhood, came a second blast on the road that separates the United Nations offices from those of the High Commissioner for Refugees. The seventeen dead from the U.N. were grisly reminders of the civil war that had already claimed 200,000 lives in this chronically turbulent country. The AQIM— Al Queda in the Islamic Maghreb— made a chilling claim: another successful conquest carried out by the Knights of the Faith with their blood in defence of the wounded nation of Islam. More recently, seventy people were wiped out in August attacks.

That night, the wind blew mysteriously, gently. A patient atmosphere absorbed all the fumes disgorged into it, receiving everything and preparing to restore freshness to the world in exchange. For what causes were people ripped apart? Questions broke the uneasy surface of sleep as the Peaceweaver tossed and turned.

And when the Peaceweaver woke, it was with a moment of disorientation that many experience as the flimsy shadows of sleep and confusion yield to the sturdy awareness of morning and wakefulness.

"Where am I?" he thought. "Am I at home or where?"

Then that first waking thought was transfixed and imprisoned by an impression stronger than the light pouring through the curtains.

He heard his own heart revving up as if on a race track. He was filled with an urgent wish to quiz those who carried out violence, thinking they were doing God a favour, those who instilled in communities of the faithful the lie that a human bomber was a martyr to be celebrated.

"Who has deceived you?" he wanted to shout. "Who has told you that God requires this, acts that rip human flesh apart along with families and their tattered dreams? Who has given you the instruction in God's name that the cause they have instilled into you with hot collective indignation necessitates this act? Can a sacred cause you have been recruited to depend on the desecration of that which is also sacred?"

He knew that the causes men killed for in God's name were deeply felt and by no means mindless. He knew, too, that the life of an Iraqi or African was no less valuable than a media-cushioned Westerner. But why had truth and political ideas trumped human beings? It was a card game he knew he had to explore to find out the rules.

30
In God's Name!

It was the dawn of the third millennium. Everywhere, the Peaceweaver was witnessing a revival of spiritual awareness inconceivable in a former time when it was widely assumed that religion was dead.

In the West, it wasn't the old time religion that was stirring. The children of the secular generation were not turning to the Church to satisfy hunger but to unconventional, D.I.Y. faith. Spirituality was taking off in a world built on technology, progress, and pragmatism, a world where the gurus were management consultants and advertisers. The memory of some other world continued to haunt our imagination. Though the main pre-occupation for many was their sports and fashions, their music and their videos; God's funeral had been premature. The idea that the physical universe was all there was had been too confining. There was a song to be sung. A spiritual dimension insisted on creeping through the concrete. The people were re-discovering that they was a spirit and not just a body, a mind, a sex instinct, or a worker. Sensing a reality greater than the material sphere of rational knowledge and of this world, they were hungry to experience it. The land of the spirit lay waiting to be discovered by people were yearning to sing like a flame aspiring, reaching upwards in search of the author of fire.

But the quest for certainty contained a dangerous and alien spawn. It was the deadly virus that had contaminated the water of the spirit for generations, the attitude to those outside the fold, outside the community, the blind inability to separate our cause from the cause of God. It was a partial sight, obscuring you to the faults on your side or the virtues of your adversaries. It was at once a virus and a deadly brew of religion and nationalism: the nation, the tribe, the cause endorsed with the stamp of God. To be self-critical was to ask too much of oneself. So, people pulled up the drawbridge, formed the lagers into a circle and let fear gain a victory.

Religious conflict thrived on a belief that each group had God on its side, that other groups were against God's truth and had to be fought. Truth was now an object, an object that became a weapon, a weapon with which to defend oneself and hurt others who saw things differently. Truth became more important than human beings.

Religious groups routinely disrespected each other, not seeing each other as people in their own right but as enemies who had to be opposed to protect God's interests, foes who had lost the colour of blood and become cardboard cut-outs, not real people.

In America, it was those who assumed that God always voted Republican, that God's truth required a strident view of life in which the doctrine of humanity burned only faintly. In Serbia, it was a Church Patriarch congratulating a dictator with tribal blood dripping from his hands for following the hard road of Christ. In Turkey it was a whole nation refusing to acknowledge their nation could possibly have committed genocide against Armenia. In Ireland, it was Catholics and Protestants who, for a generation, earnestly mixed religion and tribal politics, invoking God in order to keep communities apart and maintain the walls.

In India, it was Hindus, the BJP fostering violence in God's name. It had a vision: "Making India a Developed Nation and a Great Power, and creating an unshakeable national resolve to achieve this goal." The result was not just strident politics but virulent de-humanisation of non-Hindus who opposed.

When radical clerics sought to stir young men and women into radical action, leaving them heavy with a sense of obligation, when the logic of that action pointed inexorably towards violence being acceptable and then mandatory, where were the voices that framed the Protest and asked why they thought God had demanded such a chilling disregard for human life. It was surely blasphemous. As the Prophet Muhammad had said, "He who kills one man kills all humanity."

Sacrifice and martyrdom were part of many cultures. Often, resistance seemed all they had and violence was the language of the unheard. But O the terrible deceivers, the recruiters of the grim task, the staff officers of the lethal mission to detonate oneself and pull a hundred people limb from limb. And when a crowd gathered to help the victims, showing far more humanity than the bombers, they instructed another recruit to hurl himself into blood spattered oblivion along with the crowd. And Al'lah would calmly smile on the bomber, now promoted to the rank of honoured martyr! They had better be right, those recruiters and staff officers.

Yet, though the terrorists claimed the nervous headlines, the good news went largely unreported— like the countless Muslims everywhere who patiently endured the frustration of being tarred with the same brush as the exploiters of religion, like the Islamic scholars who wanted to dialogue with Christian scholars, or the Fatwa on terrorism from the Conference at Deobandi against this "inhuman crime." Seventy thousand Mullahs of all sects agreed to be bound by it. It was the greatest assembly of beards seen in India for a long time.[x]

But whether in Sri Lanka, Iraq, or Afghanistan, when a suicide bomber blew himself apart and intentionally killed large numbers of people at the same time, he was treating the victims of violence as being of no value, as being worthless. The act of violence was shouting at the victims that they were ripe only to be desecrated or destroyed. Violence generated by the unique fire of religion scraped the face off a victim, relegating him to a non-person.

Many battles for equality were fought and won, but there was a large battle still to be fought against divisions and conflict that come from the negative way religion was exploited to dehumanise opponents. Conservative religion everywhere, strengthening the identity of the faithful, was suspicious of those outside the faith. Writing people off who were not of our persuasion was the seed of violence.

Religion could be a profound means of affirming the value of human beings in the teeth of life. It gave the victims of violence a face and a name. So violence inspired by religion was acutely contradictory. The Peaceweaver was gripped with that vice-like contradiction. It was clear to him. New ways of living co-operatively WITH the Earth had to be found. New ways of living co-operatively ON the Earth had to be found.

31
Only a Bedouin Boy

The arrangements made for the safari in Tunisia, for a while, he paced his own balcony on the ninth floor, restlessly listening to the music that filled the night from the terrace below. He awoke to a red sunrise. It was worth paying a bit extra to connect with this slice of painted creation. If only he could chase the dawn and capture it forever.

Soon, it was a day that threatened ferocity. The sun was already bathing the day in warmth. Even at this time in the morning, the oven temperature must have been set high. Although hazy earlier, with the triumph of blue and yellow complete, nothing could stop the warmth from escalating into a heat with a dominance that would be inescapable.

Matt and his companions were bounced around in the back of a four-wheel drive jeep in a convoy that sped along the coast road. They climbed into the lunar landscape of Matmata, Star Wars country, where ranks of tourists peered curiously into the homes of trogladyte Berber women. Tourists were alien visitors from another world.

At Zaafrane, on the borders of the Sahara, the group took the statutory camel ride, courtesy of the Adhera tribe who were translating desert skills into experiences that lasted from half an hour to eight day treks for instant nomads.

"I've never experienced such fine soft sand," marvelled one of the party as they descended from their camels.

"I feel so free," thought Matt. The effect on him was compulsive and instantaneous. For a few minutes, he ran amongst the sand dunes and tumbled down their hot slopes. Dust- like sand trickled luxuriously through toes and fingers.

That night, from the grounds of a Saharan hotel, he saw a silver river of stars gleaming in its flow across the night. It was the Milky Way.

Now he was back in the tree in which he had sat as a boy. Once again, he was compelled to look up. Clouds were parting mysteriously, as if giant hands had opened the curtains. He could see forever. The sight was irresistible. Garden lights strung across the emptiness of space. Layer after layer of stars upon stars as far as the eye could see. Tiny sparks of light, as fine as rain on a windscreen at night. Fiery worlds. A torch-lit procession of silent participants whose parade stretched into endless distance. It spoke to him of his journey. Touching the darkness was a place where the brilliance of the stars shone with luminescence. He felt a surge of hope.

Matthew remembered the gaping years after Dad died and Mum was unable to handle life. Aunt Miriam told him about her own father, who came from California.

"Tell me about the stars," she would say as they plied the river together in search of breakfast.

"Those were exciting times," her father replied, warmed by soft nostalgic light. Her eyes had lit up in sparkling reminiscence. The air itself was alive as the dimensions of the cosmic architecture began to grip everyone who, like gramps, worked at Mt Wilson. Together they had set out to chart the night sky.

Like a guilty secret that he was clutching close to himself, Matthew wondered what he should do with knowledge of a cosmos that stretched on and on into the night. "Is there anything out there that corresponds to what's in here?" he pondered again.

The next day, with heat already building remorselessly, the vehicles swung off the road into open desert. In a few moments, it became clear what their drivers were aiming for. At the crest of a dune, stood a row of land-cruisers, white sentinels on a golden landscape. In four-wheel drive country, this was evidently a spot for the tourists to experience the thrills and spills of plunging over the hills of sand.

It was a sequence of images Matt was to record photographically among the corridors of his memory. He always flipped when death crossed his path. Death had been a taboo subject ever since that fateful day in Jerusalem so many years before. Vivid pictures were thereafter hung on the walls of his mind- immovable pictures, scenes of fellow travellers bouncing around in wonder and apprehension, of camera-wielding tourists, of local tribes-people hawking sandstone rock carvings and that roller coaster ride through what seemed to be a clear gap in the ranks of battered land-cruisers and tattered people. But, then came sudden transformation of emotions from pleasure to panic, cries of "watch out for the child," the crunching of gears and brakes, the insufficient turn to the right and the look of horror on a boy's face as a Toyota flew down on top of him.

Passengers screamed and doors flew open. A Bedouin boy lay crumpled and inert on the desert floor. There was nothing anyone could do, though everything was tried by the crowd that assembled from amongst the serried ranks of 4WDs and their occupants. Within two and a half minutes, the life of the Bedouin boy ran into the Sahara.

Suddenly, from amongst the tribes people standing to one side, a woman emerged. She ran to the lifeless boy and began to wail. Someone in the convoy had a satellite phone. Police and medics were summoned. People stood around listlessly, exchanging impressions. Tourists kept a respectful distance, except for Matthew.

After a while, moved by a sudden impulse, he went forward to put his hand on the shoulder of the wailing mother. Everyone else looked on in suspense, devoid of the convention that ordinary protocol would dictate. But, the woman looked round at Matt. He was confronted by a contorted expression, that of someone on a rack not accepting what had happened. For a moment, the desperate depths of her eyes drank in comfort from the European who was reaching out to her.

"What's your name?" Matt thought he asked in his best French.

"Habib," the lips moved.

The moment passed. Other Bedouin were gathering round and so were police vehicles. The jeep was all right. The driver was detained for questioning and a replacement driver sent out. It didn't matter that the safari was called off. No one was in the mood anymore. As if in a funeral procession, the three jeeps drove back to the resorts of the north.

"Habib," exclaimed Matt. "Her name was Habib."

"No," said the guide. "Habib was the name of the boy."

For the next two or three days, Matt trod heavily. He meandered round the souks but ignored the pressing invitation of numerous street traders. "Have a looksie, have a butchers," they said in mocking sales English. "How much?"

Matt could not respond to their bantering tone. He couldn't get out of his mind the face of Habib or that of the wailing woman who had stared back at him. The death of a child whom he had known and held would haunt him for many years. Of that he was sure, though the child was not his own and there was a mother, and maybe a father back there in the desert whose souls had just left for an ice palace of grief, where loneliness was riven with cold. Their sentence had only just begun.

"The death of a child is a candle blown out, just when it has started to burn," he thought. "Candle light flickers into life and burns for a while, and then the candle is snuffed and the light is no more. Of all human tragedies, the greatest of all is a song unsung."

Matt had always been a survivor, always landed on his feet. It bore upon him now that life hung by a slender thread. What was a life worth? How much for an unknown Bedouin boy? He had always been indignant that the life of an African or an Iraqi was worth less than that of a Westerner. But that was in principle. Now the need to sort out his own value and mortality was urgent and pressing.

The party returned via Karouian. Amidst Mosques and minarets, crowds of peaceful worshippers thronged this fourth holiest site in Islam. Amongst the first acts of the Arab conquerors centuries before was to build a great Mosque. Here was the world's oldest Minaret, rising thirty metres into a clear blue sky, calling worshippers to prayer five times every day for a thousand years and more. The great Mosque had been joined by forty others. To be present on a Friday was to witness a gleaming field of white bowing low before its Creator. It gave the troubled man some respite before the questions returned like a tenacious prosecutor.

He was only a Bedouin boy, but his death seemed so senseless, so pointless. What was the purpose of this absurd lolling about on planet Earth for a few short years? Why did it have to happen? A world where songs were cut short must have been proof that God was absent without leave (or had never existed except in the imagination or maybe a pleasant dream in a harsh world of nightmares). But, then he pulled himself up short. Did it make any more sense to conclude that there was nothing out there that corresponded to what was inside him? The very fact that it hurt so much showed that he was a thinking and feeling person. What was the source of his own humanity that cried out in the night? Where did that gift of outrage come from? And then involuntarily, Matt found himself playing an old film in his mind, a film whose reels had dusted themselves off and begun to play without asking.

32
Stop the Traffic!

Waiting for a lull, he moved into the road.

"Stop the traffic!" he cried out. "Stop the traffic!" But, the traffic wouldn't stop. There was no break. The deadly trade continued.

More people were in a form of slavery than the number of Africans brought across the ocean and sold in America all those years before. Slaves were people's property to be bought or sold. Slaves were spoils of war. People could become slave property through selling themselves to meet a debt- or selling their children. Slave societies were once common. But, you did not make slaves of your own people. You found people ripe to be converted into property. Like Africans.

It was Europe's sweet tooth that began the most notorious traffic in human beings. Two slaves out of three ended up in the sugar colonies, all to feed the growing demand. Betrayed by their fellow Africans, inland people living out their days were caught, caught in a net like one would catch a butterfly. Except you would treat a butterfly with more respect. People were herded towards the ship of the slaves, herded as if they were cattle, herded as if they were devoid of feelings. The one depended on the other. First construct people as animals, only semi-people. Then herd them. It's all right to convert them into property, people into animals into property. That is the deadly, de-humanising alchemy.

Eleven million humans were shipped across the Atlantic, once cattle, now sardines. But, these were only the survivors. One third died and had to be tossed overboard to join the other sardines. Survivors were sold in the slave markets like property. When no longer useful, the slave was sold on or abandoned to die. Now the former property and erstwhile sardines (previously cattle) were like an old car not worth keeping going.

Stopping the traffic was the first salvo in the struggle for human dignity. It took a terrible war to stop slavery amongst the cotton plantations of the Deep South, where it was part of a way of life. In the founding of the American Republic, slaves were included in the population count. Five eighths of a person was the rule of thumb, though to be fair that was more than a thumb.

But, men and women, boys and girls continued to be sold as property. There were as many slaves now as ever were shipped across the Middle Passage in those inhumane centuries that never quite ended. Eight million children were trapped in forms of slavery— to pay a debt, to be child soldiers, involved in pornography, prostitution, or forced into labour. Forced labour or sexual exploitation still claimed its millions— boys for forced labour, women and girls to be exploited for sexual services. Physical or emotional abuse awaited them. So did threats against their families or rape and death. Every year, three quarters of a million people were traded across international borders. Even in Britain, which had first stopped the traffic, trading in humans was still the most profitable activity for criminals... after drugs and weapons.

One in three parents in West Africa said that they could not earn sufficiently to feed their families. So, they were prepared to hand over their children to human traffickers.

"Stop the traffic!" urged the Peaceweaver as he moved in and out of the cars that day. But, the traffic continued.

33
The News Behind the News

To the passers-by, he was just a figure in the public square, playing his violin.

Before him jostled a changing kaleidoscope of living shapes, a bewildering melee of people and viewpoints, of facts sincerely held, of raw beliefs and polished convictions; here there was certainty and uncertainty, the search for order and the quest for change, the passion and the Protest.

It had been uncommonly hot but by now, the calm breeze was breaking thermal dominance, emancipating its prisoners and touching the senses with delight. Within its embrace, a few were gathering. Nearby, pigeons encircled a party of Japanese tourists, one of which stood like a scarecrow with arms outstretched and hands filled with pigeon food at 25 pence a bag. Quickly, the upper part of the visitor was covered with dark birds eager to oblige.

"Listen to the music," the Peaceweaver urged them. "We are a sophisticated generation used to computers, space probes, and discerning between the images of Hollywood. But do we know what we want and why we want it? Listen to the themes in the background, the top notes but also the under-notes. Listen to the music!" he urged them again. And in the public square, the solitary violin played its varied strains.

"What is your point?" they asked him.

From the sides, on cue, came several assistants. They proceeded to assume various positions on the pavement, stances that looked for all the world like its participants were involved in a game of twister.

"In the public square," continued the Peaceweaver, "we take up our beliefs and agendas. We massage our convictions and give vent to our differences. Here in this contested space, we polarise; we dispute; we challenge; we vote, and we sing our varied songs. But look below the surface of things, go deeper and see what it is others want, why they have adopted their position, and as if in a mirror, why you have adopted yours! What have these consumers of experiences taken into themselves that has become part of them? What concerns, what bedraggled motivations drive them on?

"Always probe the news behind the news," he urged further, "the variegated subtexts that haunt the news, the messages that lurk behind the push and pull of actions and reactions. The rest is technical questions...

"And now I tell you of the contest".

At this, two assistants moved from the side to occupy centre stage. The Peaceweaver took out a pendulum and began to swing it from side to side, at first gently then with scarcely veiled vigour. This was evidently the signal for the contestants, who began to wrestle, at first gently and then with scarcely veiled ferocity. Who would prevail, the one on the right or the left? Then they froze.

The Peaceweaver continued: "Look at the tired contest! Scratch a conservative! On my right, the contestant strives to pickle, to preserve. Holding on to your identity of the nation with all its endearing patriotism is vital. Traditional values, traditional institutions must be conserved, the social order maintained. He will not raise taxes, and he will not be soft, soft on crime or soft on our enemies. Listen to the music. Hear those notes of security, of playing it safe. He would defend us from attack. Those in charge must remove themselves for everybody's sake. Behold the protagonist of the free market that without interference will organise things better than any creaking and inefficient State body. Government is the problem. Hooray for the invisible hand! Take responsibility for your fortunes. If the bad old State does it all, you will not flourish. So down with dependency! Be self-reliant, the strewn path to dignity and the gold of self-respect. Release the creativity of the people! Let freedom ring to play our songs with minimum interference from critics and controllers!"

"Scratch a socialist! On my left," he said, turning to the other opponent, "are different priorities. He trumpets a fair struggle so no one has an unfair advantage. He is the champion of welfare, not warfare. He looks after those whose voice is unheard, those lacking in power and those that shunted to the margins. This opponent levels the ground. His is the battle for collective unselfishness, community, equality, co-operation and not competition or social discipline, for we are social beings, not individuals merely! That is the truth about ourselves, and that is where we will flourish, bound by common humanity. It is not how nature has endowed us but the way society has treated us that means we fight with one hand tied behind us. And so fairness must be restored in the struggle!"

The Peaceweaver held a pendulum that swung while the contestants sought to outwit the other in the trial of strength.

"At heart," said the Peaceweaver, "it is a different lesson about how to pan the gold of their worth. This is what makes the contest swing back and forward! So, choose you this day which competing vision you will see with and with which gold panner you will sieve. Believe that humans need security, rooted in identity— identity of nation, of unchanging things and of self-dependence and turn right! But if the itching instinct is that, if fairer circumstances burst through, humans will pan and work together for the common good, that we must give roadside assistance to the worst off, turn left!"

The crowd did not know what to make of this. They thought he was a madman, calling for new songs to play. But, the Peaceweaver took something out of a suitcase. It was a large piece of a wooden jigsaw. His words came thick and fast: "Each contestant holds one part. The overall picture will tell us where we sing our emancipated songs. The rest is technical questions for pragmatists of the world to unite in solving or to disagree until dawn! But for you," he urged, "listen to the music. Go below the surface. It is there we can meet. It is there, at the appointed place, that we will find a new way of playing our song in this public square where the gold panners can work and find their gold!"

He had one final point to make. The Peaceweaver brought out paper packets, though their contents were hidden from the people. He handed them out.

"Take!" he urged. "In this public square, there is taking of power. And there is also giving of power. Do not give power away too fast. Those who nurse and rehearse grievance give power away. Resentment hands out power. Do not indulge, or you will weaken yourself! We have reached a new moment. The economy is faltering like a house of cards. It is time for new contests, for new songs, new struggles, and new listening to the music. So, there will be a stirring amongst the graves and, for hope to rise like the phoenix, a confounding of the cynicism that rules."

34
Postcards of Poverty

India: a bewildering human drama where the scenes were changing incessantly and disturbingly. Scenes of beauty and ugliness, poverty and wealth, peacefulness and noise, luxury and squalor alternated rapidly. The contrast was profoundly unsettling. Matt and Amanda knew that they would be as affected by the encounter as any amongst the caravan of western travellers before them.

The gateway to India was Mumbai. Fifteen million people lived there amidst soaring skyscrapers and sprawling slums, fifteen million people from a bewildering kaleidoscope of backgrounds and speaking in a dozen tongues. A construction boom and a massive transfusion of people from the countryside made the old Bombay the largest city of one of the fastest growing economies in the world. And Bollywood put it on the map for culture vultures. Here, too, several years before, a terrorist explosion rocked the city. Multiple attacks on the city's transport system took two hundred lives. Then Mumbai experienced a full frontal attack. It was reported as India's "9/11". Random spraying of bullets across a crowded railway terminal, hostages taken, hotels under siege; it was a terrifying disregard of human life.

With a million inhabitants concentrated in a square mile of Shack City, the Dharavi district of Mumbai was Asia's biggest slum. Family hutments— as the locals called them— populated a low-rise wood, concrete, and iron skyline. In Shack City, a family of ten had to make do with thirty square metres of space, equivalent to a parking area in a European supermarket. If sleeping space was at a premium, there was always the brown water of the open sewer outside to camp besides. A round half the million inhabitants were dalits, untouchables, and Muslims— a rag-tag of India's poorest groups. A postcard of the old dehumanising poverty? Nevertheless the human spirit was alive and well in this land of the slumdog. Creativity hummed. Business start-ups were eager, especially if there was power and water you could rely on. Plainly, Dharavi was a site of ambiguity.

Their unexpected trip was yielding to a deeper place of memory, encounter, and power-driven emotions. An evening grown weary with the past passed through the darkest hour of the night to the youth and magic of the morning.

Conversation ranged across continents, time zones, and families. It was rather different from when Mandy had first given Matt the edited highlights of what she had passed through. A few words of exclamation were all that Matt could muster, though acutely conscious of being trifling, fumbling, utterly incapable to do justice to the encounter. He felt a pang like a toothache for the years that the locusts had eaten.

He had always had a great deal of affection for Mandy. Under the hard crust, her intense fragility echoed to the fault-lines under his own success... until he hit the buffers himself. After that, shared moments of solidarity became possible, though rarely experienced. It was the beginning of a new chapter.

Mandy was still waking up to a life in which the old patterns were rudely replaced by disorganisation. Anger, guilt, and fear cascaded through her at regular intervals. Mandy lived the zipped up life of a forty-something professional until the zip broke. But, she was pleased to accept and free to do so when, with Daniel doing well in the rehab, Matt suggested she come along on a trip to India. She no longer felt that, if she stopped holding on, death would close up above her and she would be trapped forever in the subterranean world of the dead. Now she had a lifeline to a world that she had glimpsed sometimes and knew was up there, a world of sunshine and of sky. Into that world she had emerged, literally, when they stepped off the plane at Mumbai.

Posters from the Bharatiya Janata Party adorned walls and placards everywhere. It was a militant Hindu organisation wedded to national unity, national integrity, national identity, and national strength through national character. Its fascist slogans were as fearsome as the Tiger. Violence to demonised outsiders, Christians or anyone seen to be weakening India lay only a dagger away. India was more ambitious, more self-confident, and more capable than ever before. It had initiated a space programme. It was set to become a technological and industrial giant. Yet, the status of human life was still in its infancy. One of the Hindu nationalists behind the 2002 Gujerat massacre thought that at least twenty-five thousand to fifty thousand Muslims should die. The flood defences were not yet in place.

A lengthy train journey through dry Rajastan brought them to Jaipur, its old walled quarter washed salmon-pink. Not long before, seven bombs had exploded there, another outside a Hindu temple. The push bike was being used as a carrier for terrorists. Was it Islamic Jihadists set to provoke a backlash that would radicalise India's one hundred fifty million Muslims by attacking religious sites? The jury was still out.

Another ten hours by train brought them brought them, via Agra and the Taj Mahal, to Varanasi Junction. They arrived at the ancient capital of Hindu faith and learning. Once in a life time, Hindus would visit old Benares to wash away their sins. To die here was to be most favourably placed to ensure the best possible rebirth.

"It was Mark Twain who said 'Benares is older than history, older than tradition, older even than legend and twice as old as all of them put together,' " Matt remarked to Mandy.

After checking into a low budget hotel, they sought the services of a rickshaw guide. They could have made it around by foot, but Matt said it would be good for a first time visit. A guide would stop them from being pestered by beggars and fake Sadhus after their money. And so, in the twilight world of early evening, they found themselves carted round a mysterious world populated by dope fiends, money lenders, holy men, and road side barbers. Purveyors in the silk emporium followed the traditions of centuries. When he was a royal prince Siddartha, the Buddha, had prized the silks of Benares. There was a kindliness and respect for life in the Right Speech and Right Action he had espoused. Visiting the Deer Park at nearby Sarnath would keep until next time.

Twelve million people wove using handlooms in India. Here in Varanasi, a weaving tradition was facing survival crisis. Silk had been woven in these alleyways for centuries. Once the silk capital of India, the Varanasi silk sari was a must-have item for every bride. Now, more than fifty thousand weavers were jobless. There was hardly any work now. Food had left the bowl. Michembar had lost everything. His wife and his youngest daughter had died. Now his house was gone and with it, his livelihood and his work. Changing times, trade rules and exposure to globalisation had wrecked the industry. No one was buying weaves made on handlooms now. Chinese saris woven on power looms were cheaper. Typically, weavers could earn no more than 65p a day. There was no food. Weavers were petitioning the government to push for exemption for textiles from trade rules. And so people were dying from hunger. Handlooms had become live graves.

If Matt and Mandy were lost amidst the countless bazaars and stalls, they needn't have been worrying, the rickshaw guide explained. Following a sacred cow or a funeral procession would always return them to familiar landmarks.

The wind of the night stirred fretfully against the windows of the hotel. The travellers had arranged to be woken an hour before dawn. Their guide was waiting. He pulled them in silence through winding alleys dominated by mountains of incense, fruit, and vegetables. The skyline was dominated by domes, towers, minarets, and temples by the hundreds, dedicated to Shiva, the presiding deity of old Benares. The travellers were drawn to an unforgettable kaleidoscope of temple priests, pyres of smouldering people, and old ruined temples sliding into a river. They had arrived at the Ganges.

Hindu pilgrims crowded on to the Ghats, stepped embankments along the river bank, and prepared for a ritual bath and the ceremony of Puja in praise of the rising sun. Thousands of pilgrims stood waiting for the priests to call to the dawn. Then came the redness of the rising sun and, with it, a broken silence. Ghats draped in the mistiness of early morning suddenly woke to life. The faithful flocked to the river to wash their clothes along with their sins. Pyres were being lit for the first cremations of the day. By the riverbank, sick people lay on filthy rags or mats of rattan, waiting to die. As the sun began to build intensity, Mat and Mandy were glad to pause under a tree that offered shade. They reached the market. A dozen butchers were killing animals right there on the street in their stalls. Car horns were blown addictively.

Was this India?

As they continued their journey, village after village sped past the train window. The statistics were formidable. Two thirds of its billion people lived in rural areas. Their condition was defined by lack— lack of access to financial resources, lack of the means to produce for themselves, lack of access to water, health care, and literacy. Chronic lack hung over the villages. A third of the people could not muster a dollar a day. The nations had committed themselves to halving the huge swathe of people eking out their existence on less than that. For all that, India's severe food shortages were a thing of the past. Local and regional projects abounded and the economy was accelerating. "India Rocks," the Hindustan Times famously proclaimed. Global power was definitely shifting eastward. Yet, underneath India's economic miracle lay enormous problems. Half of India's children were sufficiently malnourished, not to achieve their proper height. If one were to take five children in the world below the poverty line, two would live in India.

It was a contrast, too, with their next stop: the dusty, neglected Sitamarhi District in Bihar State, the poorest of the poor. It was a place of drought, of withered crops— not the kind of place in which one would expect to encounter girl power. Yet, here, one determined girl had transformed herself into an educated young woman. Her twin brother caught her going to school. The price was a good beating, ashamed of the fact that she dared to study when none of the men in her family had ever attended school, their mother condoned his violence. This was the unacceptable face of poverty, one of its causes.

The train rumbled on. Mandy dozed. Matt couldn't sleep. The villages flashing past, recalled his journey in Ethiopia earlier that year. A survey in 2005 showed that half the kids there were stunted, one in eight emaciated, plagued by acute malnutrition. That was de-humanising if words meant anything, worth a thousand shouts. He thought, too, of Sudan, the area between the Niles fertile land for a new colonial grab. This time it was Gulf States, prowling for food. But, what of those evicted from their land? Who would be their champion? It was profoundly and perennially disturbing.

For now it was on to Bangladesh, once dismissed by the Nixon White House as a basket case. But, just in the last ten years, one in ten of the population no longer had to go to bed with hunger pangs their constant companion. Erratic and extreme weather conspired with a low-lying area subject to a tidal rush from the Bay of Bengal framed the picture of poverty. So did the dowries. The average wage was a dollar and a half a day. A three hundred dollar dowry called down a heavy debt on a family with a girl baby who had to pay the family of a future husband. Then you had to pay for medical care to look after elderly relatives. Heartening growth had lifted people out of poverty in Bangladesh. But, social justice was a much sought after twin.

Dhaka, the site of the first gathering was home to twelve million people. Half a million of them were street kids, vulnerable to exploitation and human trafficking. Fifteen thousand girls and women were trafficked to other countries in Asia and the Middle East every year. The city was stuffed with garment factories, where thousands of women often walked two hours to work to ensure cheap clothing for the West. Sweatshop labour? An opportunity to empower women? It was ambiguous.

"So, how do we humanise the landscape," Matt wondered. And he saw individuals, standing out from postcard poverty as real people living real lives. There was Kohinoor, an urban slum dweller, demanding that her rights to basic essential services be met so that her children do not have to suffer the deprivation and pangs of hunger, which she suffered from. Would she be amongst the hundred million slum dwellers whose lives were meant to be transformed in the start-of-millennium goals?

Or how about Mozammel, a landless day labourer who remained unemployed for six months, demanded respite from money lenders to find a regular source of income? And here was Laxmi, a student from a family of city cleaners, who demanded rights to education and a life of dignity. Muslim community groups were very supportive. Green shoots studded the fertile landscape.

They travelled south, from Dhaka towards the Delta, increasingly using dirt roads burdened by women and children with their feet bare, their heads laden with water jugs or wood for fuel. It was a triumph that many women now wanted fewer children. Their destination was a village association. It was a scheme funded by the Bangladeshi Rural Advancement Committee. The women were given several hundred dollars and cheap loans from the Grameen Bank to get a small business off the ground. It was transforming the countryside, a countryside where four out of five had less than half an acre to work with. Much had been accomplished. There was much still to do amidst the eighth most populous country in the world. The old dehumanising poverty still imprisoned a third of the people in extreme poverty.

And then it was back to Dhaka, where Mandy waited for the Biminair flight to the U.K. They spoke for ages. They spoke about Sarah. Then they embraced. Matt waited for the flight to Yangon. That was a country that recognised the face of poverty. Three quarters of the people lived in rural villages. Five million Burmese faced chronic hunger. The country used to be known as the rice bowl of Asia. It was the opposite direction in more ways than one. Myanmar would be dangerous. Tight-lipped people lived there. It would not welcome anyone wanting to make contact with human rights activists.

35
In a Different Direction?

At the same time that the universe was expanding and human significance shrinking, a new and comprehensive vision was emerging of people who could not live with significance. The struggle was costly and confusing— costly, for there was much to bolt people and prevent them from rising up in protest—confusing, for people did not know what song of protest they were singing and how the words went. Gradually, scattered notes began to form a pattern: "Hang a label round each other's neck. Let the label read: 'Handle with care.' Remove the false labels of names and boxes that allow you to treat another person as second class freight."

Countless battles were fought for the dignity and worth of humanity. "Hang a label round their necks. Treat them with value (for there's something special about human beings)." It drove the contemporary agenda, the struggle for equality, dignity, and justice. A new vision... or an old one dressed differently?

Loud indignant protests arose against show trials without recourse, committing their victims to prison or institution, the continuing traffic in people, the struggle of the disabled wanting society to relate to them as an individual, the struggle of women to be empowered, and the battle for equality in the work. For centuries, Western society was unsure about how to treat women. But, a new world was coming.

There were those angry voices raised against the economics of the day before yesterday. "Don't measure our value by money... Tell the whole story about us." In any enterprise, the crucial ingredient was still the human ingredient: the morale, the participation. Where people had incentives to work and the freedom to do so, wealth was created, value that they found in themselves transmuted mysteriously into gold.

"Human beings are only a set of chemicals... nothing but a group of neurons... nothing but a selfish gene... a number." As if everything to be said had been spoken, the mystery flushed out. Such explanations left abandoned orphans bereaved of joys and sorrows, loves and laughter, memories and ambitions, their identity and their freedom of choice, their purpose and their meaning. "Don't they know how valuable you are?" - "Hang a label round their necks. Handle with care."

On every side, a crescendo arose against the injustice. "Speak up for those who cannot speak for themselves, for the rights of all who are destitute. Speak up and judge fairly; defend the rights of the poor and needy." It was loud; it was defiant! The tragedy of the violence and the victims of the violence weighed heavily upon the world— those who felt of little worth themselves, tearing it from their victims, to take and scrape what they had never had and leave them degraded. The last years of the millennium were an era of unstable currencies, but devaluation of humanity ran on and on behind the scenes, an identical twin to discrimination. Wherever people were disregarded, their sense of worth trampled on, treated as an object, or a rude play thing for others, then prejudice and devaluation gloated over its victims, raping and stripping them of their value along with their clothes.

Devaluation was the indifference, the jokes that people told against each other, making fun at another's expense. Devaluation was one robbing oneself, the low self-worth that hung its head in shame-filled response to another's words. It was children making fun of each other on the school playground, the constant put-downs of one person by another, bullying and character assassination in the work place, criticisms what people were and what they did. They measured ones value by money, by exam performance, by status, by the job. And from all of these encounters, humans walked away reduced in size, instantly dwarfed. Why did it hurt so to be re-constituted as only two feet tall? Could people give a reason why they hated to be ignored or explain what it was about people that made them think that they were worth something? Millions felt oppressed by class divisions and the put-downs. "You're less of a person, because you're not one of us!" The hierarchy of occupation was expelling a hierarchy based on wealth and privilege. Class was breaking down. Media exposed the foibles of the aristocracy or the pretentiousness of the rulers. Formality was stuffy. Informality was in. But pockets of old attitudes hang over the world like relics, angry relics. Anti-Semitism and white supremacy was the virulent plague that still erupted in coarse, malign influence like a diseased pus. Racism scraped value from human beings, though a fact of life and an institutional in-built devaluation. How much longer would skin-deep colour assign first and second and sometimes third class citizenship to human beings? There arose an angry protest. White, yellow, black, brown had equal worth. "Don't they know how valuable you are?" - "Hang a label round their necks... Handle with care".

But amidst the darkness, there was the flame of many candles where respect was given and kindness ruled. In every walk of life, an atmosphere based on mutual respect and imparting value to another person made for a relaxed, orderly environment, where human beings could do their best work. What ultimate realities determined that people could thrive where individuals were taken seriously.

THE SIXTH LANDSCAPE
Demonisation

"There are different ways to look upon the inmates of prisons and jails in the United States. One way is to look upon them as members of a different species, indeed as a type of vermin, devoid of human dignity and entitled to no respect; and then no issue concerning the degrading or brutalising treatment of prisoners would arise." - Judge Richard Posner, a U.S. Judge [xi].

"The other non-Jewish workers used to joke when the smoke from the crematorium blew our way. 'They're burning pigs again today.'" [xii]

"Who's going to remember all this riff-raff in ten years time? No one." - A remark from Stalin to Yezhov, his KGB chief, signing the latest list of people to be executed. [xiii]

"I like people who are ours. I don't like those ones because they are Orangemen. They are bad people" - a Catholic, aged 4

"The I.R.A. and Catholics shoot people and wear masks." - a Protestant girl, aged 5 [xiv]

36
Shooting Rabbits in the Mountains

He could not get out his mind the sheer-sided mountain in Bosnia. As he continued his journey, a luxurious landscape yet again awakened wonder from deep within him. He stopped beneath falling water that disburdened her load into a lake. On one side of him, a green mountain was arraigned in layers. On the other side, mountains rose straight up above the lake in easy dominance. Woods crowded upon woods, hills surrounded hills and groves of trees were clothed with the sun. In the flush of a new day, life surged through meadows that carpeted the valley and echoed in the wooded slopes of hill and mountain. Craggy peaks shone with the morning.

Below him, the Drina river ran to the sea. Long before, it had cut a path of least resistance. He could just make out where it fell with a sheer drop that dashed unsuspecting water to pieces. As he tuned his ears to the sound, it seemed to him as if he could make out the water splashing as it had on the very first morning. There was a time when Earth had just been born. An atmosphere was gathering. Giant taps poured water for days, water that laughed and played and splashed for the sheer joy of being alive. Salty oceans were formed, circling the globe.

"We live," he exulted, "in a world filled to overflowing with water, water sparkling, flowing, roaring, alive with strength and speed, fury and joy!"

Here was no picture postcard of mass-produced scenery, but living mountains, trees that clapped and, to the right a lake that glistened with colour as the sun's shadow raced across the waters.

"A mountain is not just a mountain!" he exclaimed.

He had been here before; memories that interpreted the raw material spread out before him that added layers of meaning and significance. A sense of place had been fashioned. The Peaceweaver wanted to jump into the picture. Every landscape begged to be noticed, to be enjoyed. For a while he could do nothing but gaze at the mountains, the trees, and the lake until they began to vanish from his thoughts, though still present to sight. Entranced in his reverie, the music within formed a song that slowly liberated itself into being like a touch of spring filling the air or a child being born. Appreciation was a shared experience to enjoy, so today he invited the mountains to sing along.

And in that moment of praise-filled rapture, he understood that whoever had felt the inspiration of the mountains, the call of the wild place, or the intrigue of the sea had touched an undisclosed sense of something that transcended the ordinary. Through a rich tapestry of memory that added layers of meaning to the landscape, there was yet another layer without which its full significance died unheard. A song assembled on his lips, leaping upwards.

But all too quickly, the song of wonder was marred. The mountain spoke once more with a sand-paper abruptness that jarred every nerve.

"Your daughter is good for wife!" the mountain said.

An earthquake had come and gone. Fault lines had opened up between communities who had lived side by side for peaceful centuries. Serbian soldiers had organised a rape factory in their barracks in Bosnia. Women were reluctant to share their stories of the ultimate shame in Muslim society. If pregnant, they faced a miserable future of rejection by their families, raising a child conceived in hatred.

The Peaceweaver shuddered at the memory of a young woman, scarcely older than a teenager, who had come to Britain in those days. They forced her father to watch as the Serbs threw her to the ground and ripped off every part of her clothing. Her neighbours didn't understand why she now woke up at night screaming. In her mind was etched the torture that contorted her father's face before she fell into his arms.

His face creased. What was it that Bosnian woman pleaded with him? "Tell someone that we are worth fighting for. We are people, not animals for the slaughter or dogs for their sport."

The mountain saw and heard it all. In mute testimony, it witnessed the terrible day when eight thousand Muslims were forced into trucks, brought to the Drina and shot. Lying amongst the dead, a survivor recalled the soldiers talking. "That was a good hunt. There were a lot of rabbits here." [xv] In this part massacre, part blood sport, humans were converted into animals. It was always like this. Call someone a rabbit (or worse) and one could treat them like something worse than a rabbit. Rabbits could be dangerous. The Muslims of Srebenicia had become dangerous. Or good for wives.

37
The Next Train to Utopia

Through the massive steel and glass structures covering them, the Byzantine Clock Tower cast a lengthy shadow over the platform of the Kiyevsky Rail Terminal. He watched for a while across its marble floor as the giant screen paraded imminent departures to Athens, Istanbul, Belgrade and Prague. The Rome train was not shown yet. It was delayed. From what he could make out, the incessant announcements were not giving much away. The Peaceweaver strolled for an hour on the nearby Moskva river, its gentle surface coloured by a late afternoon sun. He went back. Still no sign.

Two cups of coffee later, he paced up and down the Moscow platform. He read a plaque on the wall. When the station was planned, they felt peace and prosperity had dawned. There would be a flowering of the arts, of the sciences. Some bemoaned decadence but artists, writers, philosophers, and everyone else were filled with exciting possibilities. Relativity, psychology, sociology, and Marxism were radical theories that went hand in glove with a future filled with planes, cars, wireless and electricity. Science and reason were driving the progress train, fuelled by noble optimism about our capacity to achieve a better world. Anything was possible. The world was conquered, the Titanic unsinkable. The Tsar still ruled Russia in those days. Then the First World War slaughtered its millions. Wild-eyed Bolsheviks arrived with fire in their minds. By the time the Tsar was killed, the station was complete.

As he continued his journey, asking questions, he was tuning into the songs of humanity. Many songs had been played in the century that was drawing to a close, songs mighty in their influence— modern versions of reality, big symphonies with large gaps in the music. All such songs seemed to have been incomplete, baffled by the radical evil that people did. They were powerful, compelling dreams.

The communist dream had now virtually been driven out of business, a hopeful story that tried to paint the whole picture but failed so starkly. In the darkness of the night, shadows arose. The dreamers of Communism hoped that people were good and power would not be abused. It was to have been paradise regained, a hopeful place where landowners and factory owners would be swept away, a place in the sun where equality had arrived. But instead, a chasm of darkness opened up. A flawed dream completely ignored the possibilities of evil. And so, few people were now standing round to see this big picture in the political exhibition. They had moved on to smaller pictures and smaller dreams. But at what cost! Both Communism and Fascism, its evil twin, generated a tragic waste of life. Lenin's body no longer remained embalmed in Red Square. It had passed into history, the death of an ideal, a golden age that was no longer golden, a dream fatally flawed. It was a symphony of hope through social conflict but now only nostalgic revolutionaries were listening.

It left the running of the perfect society in the hands of imperfect men. Like the Kims of North Korea who had kept their country in abject poverty, its ideology a smoke screen for a sordid, failed state. Like Mao, a warlord totally indifferent to the death of millions, radically contemptuous of life, or of enemies of the people. There were so many people, China could afford to lose them. Like Pol Pot, a sad little man who had turned Cambodia into a killing field. Professional people of any sort— teachers, doctors, and intellectuals— all had to be exterminated for society to be rebuilt. A nightmare experiment in social engineering led to genocide and the death of two million of his own people. Even Mao did not kill a quarter of the population.

In the 80's and 90's, cynical passive spectators rose up with one voice and quickly swept it all away. The system had failed to attend to the needs of its people. The song failed, shown up at last in its incompleteness, a song blind and naive to the evil that men did, a song grey and drab because it did not sing to createdness or take account of a Zhivago in love, an individual against the system. Apparently, people didn't function well unless they felt their little lives counted. Someone should have told Marx. It was meant to be utopia by the next train.

"Take up a lament for the broken dreams, the forlorn hopes of individual happiness, soft dreams and pillowed utopias," the Peaceweaver had said in the Moscow gathering.

"Human life has been cheap at the price in Russia. Build up your defences," he urged them. "Build up your defences against invasions of the sacred life of your people. Guards Divisions can learn to mount patrols over that which erodes the dignity and vulnerable value of humanity. We fail to grasp the dilemma at the heart of things. Believing that the sins of the world are only what others have done to us, we are condemned to limited vision. Trapped in innocent naiveté, thus secure against open secrets, we will refuse to believe the stories of what left or right— or your own people— did. We waited for the train that never came.

The end of the experiment had come upon humanity. For decades, the story had been told and the assumptions made. The only hindrances were external and destructive patterns, or so it was said. But despite countless manifestos, why were we not more at peace and more content? What was holding up the train? It was long overdue. The far side of hope was dark... very dark. It was hardly the beginning of the demonisation. But, it was the end of dreams.

Suddenly, his reverie was pierced by an announcement. An apology preceded the arrival of the train. People scurried to find a seat. Cases and baggage were loaded. Within hours, they were witnessing the deceptively soft looking surface of a snow mountain beside the track.

Distant white mountains were awake that night and seemed to be moving. Wind-polished ice gleamed in the lights of the train. Freezing fog enveloped the track ahead. He began to sleep. Sleep yielded to dreams, images of the night, playing and pulling on his mind. People can't be trusted with dreams. O the white-carpeted utopias trampled on and stained with mud and blood! O the hopes, daubed with graffiti! Who was responsible for undermining dreams because the men of violence had another dream in their eyes?

In his dream, he was walking endlessly down a corridor draped with snowy white sheets, journeying towards a world where those with fire in their minds finally learned to give value to slaughtered innocents and dreams did not descend into nightmares.

38

Dear Steve,

You must, no doubt, have heard that I am in Burma. They're holding us.

The Army believes it must stay in power, that no other group or party can hold the country together and run it efficiently. Many people are saying that, worn very thin in the wake of the cyclone that has brought death, destruction, and disaster to the country. The continued detention of the well-known political prisoner, the Nobel Peace Prize Laureate Daw Aung San Su Kyi, is a blot on the political landscape. The Junta has introduced a roadmap to democracy but, at the same time, continues to hold more than a thousand political prisoners. I took part in a protest. I gave an interview to a paper, in which I said that the Junta seemed more interested in looking after itself than its people, that it did not value the human. Next day, I was bundled into a car and taken to await trial.

As soon as I emerged from the gleaming marble of Yangon airport, I knew that posing as a tourist wasn't really an option for me if the self-censorship that local people have with foreigners ever began to break down. Giving people a voice is alluring. Sule Pagoda was thronging with worshippers that day, alive with Monks in saffron robes. Worship is one form of resistance that is always open to the Burmese. Its Buddhism is invariably non-violent. I guess that I was lulled by the absence of police.

But the police are inside people's heads. It was the young people who seemed ready for change, and they were in the forefront of the demonstrations. This is after all the generation that frequents internet cafes, where images of Protest are flashed around the world. A group of young people dispelled the image that I had of a tight-lipped country. They didn't believe that the world outside was constantly peddling lies. In spite of itself, Myanmar is opening up to the outside world.

That was two months ago. One thing they are allowing me to do is write a letter home. Of course it's going to be vetted, but there is a condition: I can write to you once a month as long as I don't further criticise the regime.

This I have agreed to, as there is a task for which I need your help. I've been allowed to keep my notebook. In it I have recorded impressions and conversations to do with my journey over the past few years, endeavouring to weave peace. I read lots over those years, endlessly making notes on what I have been thinking about.

It's like I have been given a lens. I want to try to put together what I have seen and heard on my journey. For ten years, I have been thinking hard, re-constructing events that I have witnessed, searching for patterns and making connections like any counsellor or, come to that, novelist teasing out significance from the chaotic stream of daily events. For ten years, I have been an intent watcher and listener, in the fray and of it, woven from the same cloth as everyone else yet with this daring search for the source of our value. I am now ready to write down my thoughts. Would you do the job of editing and seeing if there is anything in this rag tag collection that could be published?

Maybe it needs the melange of music and epic drama that you find here— zat pwe they call it. Rural villagers, especially, are drawn to it. The entire community comes out to watch. This is where young people learn community values. But, all I have is a notebook of stories, jagged memories, and a thousand hopeful impressions.

On a personal note, I am all right generally, though the old prostate problem seems to be returning. I don't know, except the calls of nature are somewhat difficult in this cell with others. I spare your blushes. Through an interpreter, I hear many stories of the other inmates. Some of them— many of them— have AIDS. The tales told beat a movie any day and other sources of entertainment hands down.

I have another favour, and one that you may find interesting or nauseous, depending on your point of view. Free from incessant travelling, what grabs my attention more and more is what happened to us both, the stream we both swam in until the currents of our lives took us on divergent courses. I've been thinking much more about Jerusalem and the way that shaped us so profoundly. Mandy has filled you in, hopefully, about how this was stirred up for me following the death of a boy in Tunisia a year ago. I wanted to seek out the parents, but I was waiting until after the trip to Myanmar. I sometimes find myself wondering about the family of the terrorist who did what he did. Through a friend in Israel, I put an advert in one of the Arab papers in Jerusalem. There may be replies by now for all I know in the in-box of my computer. Could you check it?

Thanks very much. Please give my love to Liz. Take care of yourself and write soon.

39
Jerusalem

Alone with his memories lies the sleeping man. His mind, though shut down like a quiescent fire, nevertheless stores the remembrance of experiences past. Tattered memories and broken dreams, experiences framed in bright lights, experiences heavy with regret, all jostle together in the mind of the sleeping man like faces in a crowd. A hundred whispers, a conspiracy of sadness and joys stir hauntingly through the watches of the night. Heartache, longing, and despair are mixed into the same potion as laughter, lightness, and joyfulness. The sleeping man drinks and drinks.

And when he wakes, it is with a moment of disorientation that many experience as the flimsy shadows of sleep and confusion yield to the sturdy awareness of morning and wakefulness. "Where am I?" he thinks. "Am I at home or where?" Then that first waking thought is transfixed and imprisoned by an impression stronger than the light pouring through the cell of his prison. "That was no dream".

Two communities in conflict— the one impelled by security, the other motivated by self-respect and the desire to assert itself away from the stifling de-humanisation and control.

Israel. May 1971. It was the last day of the school trip.

In Jerusalem, the six day war had lasted barely half that as Israeli paratroops encircled East Jerusalem and the

Old City. By the end of June '67, the Israeli government had declared the reunification official. Jerusalem was annexed. A new phase of Palestinian nationalism had begun. Guerrilla organisations were formed. Despite that, Jerusalem was changing quickly. The Jewish quarter was being rebuilt. New neighbourhoods were being thrown up around the city to make repartition physically impossible. Safe enough, it was assumed, for a school trip to Israel to go ahead.

The party of twenty-six boys spent two days in Tel Aviv, two days in Galilee, and a day at Masada. Via the snake path, the boys climbed up to the fortress. It was fifty degrees centigrade. The old ruins of Masada resonated with the last ditch resistance of its defenders and their decision to put each other to death rather than let themselves be taken.

In the culmination at Jerusalem, most of the sites were included in the itinerary. The last day began with a walk along the Rampart on top of the Old City Walls. Under expert tutelage, the boys saw the Western Wall, the last remnant of the Jewish Temple. The Dome of the Rock and the Temple Mount looked out mysteriously on the Jewish quarter to the west and the Arab quarter to the north. Through the Old City, then they retraced the pathway of Jesus on the way to crucifixion. It was while walking down the Via Dolorosa that a group of the schoolboys muttered mutiny and conspiracy.

"How many more sights are we going to see?" Matt could still hear himself groaning.

"It's doing my head in, all these places of interest," said Steve with usual melancholy.

"I'm bored," agreed Bill, their companion. "I don't want to stay at the hotel for another of those talks put on by old Jarvis," he said, disgusted. "Fancy doing that to us on our last night!"

"Look. How about doing something? Arranging our

own plans?" said Steve. And so it was agreed.

They would go off in search of adventure that evening. A bar? A nightclub? This was their last night in Israel. Let whatever come that would come. Mr Webber, father to Matt and Steve and teacher in charge of their group, would, no doubt, kick up a stink. But deep down, he would understand. They could explain after if caught. They plotted to slip away after the evening meal at the hotel. No one would notice. Their Dad would assume that they were up in their room and wouldn't come looking for a while.

The boys wandered through a Jewish quarter that whispered elusive mystery. Through the Arab quarter and the Damascus Gate they went, in search of a nightclub and adventure that was proving unexpectedly tantalising. They passed the Wailing Wall, still thronged with those who placed slips of prayer in its cavities. And there, near the Jaffa Gate, they found themselves in a bar and stayed there for a while. Steve purchased some cigarettes from a market stall. They sat there, puffing away, seeming to have found the trap door that emerges into adult life.

It was 9.45 when their adult reverie was shattered. Their father was looking at them through the window of the bar. There was no escape. He had come for them. "I'll deal with you later" he said, as he frog-marched them along the road and then made a fateful decision. They would return to the hotel by bus.

As these scenes moved by his memory like an old film, poignant with tear jerking emotion, Matt wanted to run to the front of the cinema screen in his mind and say, "Stop the film. Stop the film," as if he was hailing down a taxi. What would anyone do if they knew they had only four minutes to live?

In slow motion, he saw the face of a terrorist appear at the entrance of the bus and a small object of terror thrown to the back where the boys sat. To his dying day, Matt would remember horror erupting volcanically. There was no escape. Roll the film on two eternal seconds and he saw his Dad throwing himself onto the grenade. "NO, NO, STOP THE FILM." It took an age for the grenade to go off. The look on his father's face was that one that he saw when he shaved some mornings. For one long, lingering moment, the boys watched, transfixed by the volcano horror that had engulfed them from nowhere. Statuesque, rooted by terror, they looked at their father, and he looked at them, the face of their conscience forever.

Matt looked up at the film.

"Will Dad, please, reappear? Whose is this thick red sticky blood moving over us?"

He saw a bustling street erupting into chaos. He saw dozens of screaming people showered with glass, the air filled with black smoke and sharp with the smell of an explosion; he saw bystanders running and shouting.

Steve had to have glass shards removed from his leg. A passer-by endeavoured to stem the blood with his handkerchief. They all went temporarily deaf with the loudest noise that they had heard before the silence descended. Thankfully, miraculously, the boys suffered minor injuries.

"How that incident shaped my life," thought Matt as he finally stopped the film. The man in the cell with him was stirring. "The Romans believed that, if someone's name is on someone's lips, he is still alive. Dad is still alive somewhere," he whispered.

40
Call in the Accountants

The Peaceweaver recalled the tomb of Napoleon at Hotel des Invalides in Paris. Confronted by defeat, the Emperor of the French had said, "A man like me cares little for the lives of a million men. I may lose the throne, but I shall bury the whole world in its ruin." Two million were killed in Napoleon's battles. But, that was nothing compared to what was looming on the horizon. The First Great War cost nine million lives. The terrifying disparity between the scale of the slaughter and the aims for which men had marched to war haunted Europe for two generations. The war that followed reaped a terrible harvest of fifty million people destroyed. And still it went on. And on. Until the final battle.

During the last half-millennium, more than one hundred major wars had been fought in Europe alone. The pattern of war continued into the last years of the twentieth century. What were they fighting for? What causes claimed the destruction of life?

The sights and sounds of more recent wars came alive to him. Nuclear terrorism had grown nearer. Like an enormous mushroom cloud, the shadow still hung with gaunt shame over the world.

In the last year of the old millennium alone, ten wars between nations and twenty-five internal conflicts had ravaged human life. Forty-eight million people had suffered or died in the wars of the world that year. Hopes that world peace and a new age would come since the millennium were dampened by reality. Seventy-seven wars stalked the world now, seventy-seven wars with their brutalising cold reality and hissing hot blood, seventy-seven wars de-humanising friends and demonising enemies.

There were signs of hope. They were being honest about that dirty war in Argentina, in Chile... some of them were, at least. A thirty year war had come to an end in Northern Ireland. What cause demanded four thousand lives? What game was it that trumped such de-humanising loss and the crowded acts of violence?

In East Timor, two hundred thousand people were killed over the years in a territory that grew little more than coffee. On his journey, the Peaceweaver remembered vividly the queue in Colombo, where the people were ordered to register in an effort to track their origins. "A trade-off on my dignity," a student had said, having been served with toffee and sweet drinks. They wanted to find out those who had links with the Tamil Tigers. Two hundred Tiger cadres had been killed the week before, so they said. For the sake of a separate homeland, seventy thousand had died in a twenty-five year war. Twice that number had been displaced in recent fighting, all for the sake of a separate homeland. It better had been worth it! It better had justified the loss of the elephants!

But no accountant could be spared to draw up the balance sheet. The human cost of war, unknown civilians, and unknown elephants would not enter on to the ledger.

And then there was Congo. Amidst the dense jungle, it was as if the entire population of Denmark had died in ten years. (That's forty-five thousand dead each month.) It wasn't just the red scenes of battle. Civil war had disrupted a nation and its access to proper health care and proper food. Thousands were forced from their homes. Armed Groups demanded that child soldiers be recruited, released, then re-recruited. Some were killed pour encourager les autres. Women were raped on a scale that was beyond human telling. Half the dead were children, children under the age of five. They never knew the causes for which the candle flame was extinguished so prematurely.

War was all diabolical, of the devil. War evoked the noble and the heroic, self-sacrifice, extraordinary acts of courage, organising ability, tactical cleverness, strategic insight, loyalty, and comradeship. But, it was profoundly de-humanising. What war did to friends, enemies, and the dark corridors of oneself distorted people like shapes in the hall of mirrors. Conflict was often a lesser of evils, but it's causes were those familiar in everyday life; the conquest, the greed, the cruelty, the pride and the envy projected onto a larger canvas on which we painted.

The images of a world in conflict exploded in the Peaceweaver's face. The end of the Cold War brought some relief to the world but only changed the pattern. The world arms trade wouldn't stop growing, like a cancer in the body politic. What was wrong with people? How did it happen that fifty times more was spent on arms and armaments by developing countries than on health and education? How was it that more than three hundred thousand lives every year were ended with conventional weapons? There was a firearm for every ten people on the planet. Did people need so many? Was it always going to be like this?

The Peaceweaver was disturbed. Did he have to live in a world scarred by war and violence? The mark of Cain was strong, rude, and clear. Red scenes of war and addiction to violence stained a blue and white planet. The scent of blood was strong.

"The whole earth is burdened down and set to break with the weight of our violence," he thought. "The bloodiest century since the world began forces us to confront a dark inner secret under the surface. And still it runs wide and runs deep. Where shall we go to paint the unleashing of the primeval darkness? On the never neglected battlefield, I have stared at the dead faces of those who grinned back, faces that could have died laughing rather than screaming, faces that had had live eyes staring out from them only a few hours before. These are eyes that will haunt me until the end, eyes that follow me about and ask, 'Why?' A face that gazes with a curious mix of accusation and wistfulness, a face that wonders what has happened to the mysterious entity inside we call a person?

"Come and smell the lurid aroma of a woman's guts hanging out, the putrid whiff of excrement mixed with blood. Come with me to mangled remains of damaged vehicles, bloodied limbs, victims crying for help, and billowing smoke where the air is thick with the smell of burnt human flesh after the explosions and cries of distress. What causes justify the desecration of the innocent?

"Hear the muted voices of women, now silent, who clung to their children and screamed at the soldiers to spare them. Hear the soldiers who were at first disturbed by the killing and then accepted it. "It's okay to kill them. That's what you are supposed to do!' Everywhere I have heard the terrible sound of men marching to war and witnessed a hundred ways and weapons for destroying people, grisly in their silent presence. Take up a lament for the unwilling civilians, for the women with their children!

"What is it about us that we will stop at nothing to enforce our causes?" pondered the Peaceweaver. "Fighting the external foe, we are betrayed by the enemy within. It is time to face the causes as well as the consequences. It is time to ask and weigh in the scales the political utility of war. It is time to call in the accountants to match the price tag against the cause we fought for. Only then will the illusion of a positive balance sheet be broken. Only then will the stark, demonising futility put its hand up to be counted, to be subject to public disgrace."

41
What Am I Bid?

And then there was walk round the city. Visiting Paris was always like greeting a well-known friend. But, there was something different today that lent a prophetic quality to an ordinary walk. This time, he had his eyes open.

Since the beginning of the third millennium, he had been on a journey, taking stock of the value of human stock around the world. The global financial crisis towards the end of his journey had sent economic value reeling and descending, spiralling down. But what was the value of human stock in the emotional and political transactions of the world?

This was where it had all begun. Back in twelfth-century France, the first brokers were trading in debt and government securities. By the early 1700s, Paris was a fully operational stock exchange. The fourteen columns of Le Palais de Bourse propped up the economy. The Bourse was fully electronic now, but not so long before, it had been an open-outcry exchange where traders and brokers jostled on the floor. In the old days, only licensed Agents de Change could operate.

In the gallery, it was not hard to imagine the hustle of those days. The tourists around him began to fade out as the Peaceweaver was lost in the imaginary clamour. He saw a melee of Agents de Change moving brusquely across the floor in their clamour to find intermediaries for their stock. Ties were flapping amidst pin-stripe suits. Mobile phones were glued to their ear but their eyes were glued to a giant screen where numbers flashed in beguiling frenzy. "What am I bid?" they would demand in their specialist vocabulary, a language game that was a mystery to outsiders. Clearly, market crashes had been taking place across the world, and this was no exception.

There had been a slight recovery the previous day, but the fall was increasing. The feverish floor of the Exchange was a scene of the wildest excitement. Shouts of the brokers seeking to unload their stock at any price could be heard in the streets.

Something was happening on the screen. The traders jostled, bustled, and hustled in an effort to obtain a clear view. An air of anticipation hung over the floor of the Bourse like an autumn mist. New stock was being released. The value surged for a while and then, dropped back and dropped back. The slide produced audible gasps from the traders. They couldn't believe the price could be so low. They rushed across the floor shouting. But too many were selling. Speculators were making on the transactions, excitedly pointing out that the issue was over-valued to begin with. Would there be a slump? Where was the price going to settle? The global economy was collapsing like the house of cards he lovingly constructed in his boyhood.

The fall was so rapid that a conference of leading bankers had been hastily arranged. A re-assuring statement was issued. It had a temporary rallying effect in certain quarters, but still, the liquidation continued. As even this stock was depreciating, many were turning to gold. At least that held its value.

As the Peaceweaver listened more closely, he had to sit down, utterly appalled. Les Agents de Change were trading in human stock! "How much for a life?" they demanded. The answer disturbed him deeply. Anguish had crept into him that screwed his thoughts up and contorted his feelings with pain. It was all there on a screen that commanded anxious glances from the traders. The price of human stock had been rising in some years, in others it had fallen sharply and was worth little. The graph said it all. By now the great majority of small speculators had gone home, vowing never to speculate again. The bottom had dropped out of the market. The contagion was spreading around the world.

It was clear, too, from the screen that the value differed across the exchanges of the world. Life was cheaper elsewhere. In Africa, in China, it seemed like the value was on the floor. "How much for a life?" Les Agents de Change insistently demanded.

He began to walk up and down in agitation, watched by a tourist who gazed at him with consternation. He was unable to shake off the impressions that bore upon him as if he had been left holding a heavy chair but was forbidden to lay it down. For a long time that night, he defied sleep, a prisoner of his insight. And when eventually sleep was robbed no more and he slipped out of consciousness, his mind was still active, running, reeling. And in the twilight world, where shadows and voices came and went and assumed temporary shapes that dissolved on touch, what he had glimpsed leered back at him. "What price for your life?" it demanded.

For a while, a sense of impending doom and abrasive sadness gripped him. How to comprehend this blaring, difficult chorus in the music of the world was something he would struggle with until the end came. Then he felt a surge of hope. People had realised the situation. Concerned interventions were made. Numerous Change Agents had joined the melee, adding their voices to the clamour, investing, buying and raising levels of confidence that sent the stock up. Human value was on the rise!

42
Why?

Where are we, Mummy?
I don't know.
Why are we here?
I don't know.
Why are those men laughing?
I don't know.
Where are our clothes?
I don't know.
Where is my Daddy?
I don't know.
Where is my Brother?
I don't know.
Why is it dark?
I don't know.
What's that noise?
I don't know.
Why is she screaming?
I don't know.
What's that smell?
I don't know.
Why does it burn?
I don't……………………!!!

Gary Ward

THE SEVENTH LANDSCAPE
Dedication

A demonstration in Durban in the Apartheid years of South Africa. Policemen chased demonstrators. Amongst them was a black woman who dropped her shoe. The policeman intending to beat her was also an Afrikaner who had been brought up to believe that when a woman loses her shoe, you pick it up for her. He did so, automatically. Their eyes met. Suddenly, clubbing her was no longer an option. [xvi]

"It is better to light a candle than to curse the darkness." - Chinese proverb

43
Swimming and the Art of Politics

Dear Steve,

    That is fantastic news! It has blown me away, and I keep reading and re-reading your letter. When I opened it, I danced across my cell, to the amusement of my cellmate!
    You actually went to Israel, to Jerusalem! You had located the very family of the man who threw the grenade! What were they like? What did they say? I don't know what emotions are uppermost as I write— admiration or gratitude. But, then this is your story, too. You are exemplifying what it means to be a Peaceweaver. You have re-imaged the human landscape for us both, converting demons back into humans. Of course, I want to hear all about it and what was said. What on Earth did the family make of you and why you were doing it? What was going on inside you as you faced all that?
    It will be from such acts that fresh sight is given, vision that enables us to distinguish between acts and their motivations, between people and the stereotypical image they wear, between cause and effect. I am glad, too, that you did not go there as the supplicant but with a real desire to find out who had committed the act that has defined us so strongly and try to understand him. It reminds me of the restorative justice programmes that are increasingly adopted. It echoes, too, the many green shoots I have witnessed in the Middle East— Israeli and Arab children educated in the same school, Palestinians and Israelis in an orchestra. While each side holds so firmly on to Israeli

West Bank settlements or the Palestinian right of return, a two-state solution is as far away as ever. But, re-imaging the human landscape, learning to see the other side as people with similar types of motivations can only be good news for communities in conflict.

As Longfellow said, "My enemy is the friend whose story I have not yet heard."

"I don't like Mr…" Abraham Lincoln is reputed to have said. "I must try to get to know him better."

So, this is absolutely great news. At its heart, the hundred years' war between Arab and Israelis has led to the denial by either side of the right of the other to be a people, to have a narrative. They completely disregard their feelings, their reaction and the validity of their story. There will be no peace until that denial is addressed. Maybe such recognition will only come through small acts of personal encounter.

"Go below the surface," I urge people. "It is there we can meet." We must all become swimmers. Only there can we begin to understand each other. The surface is too busy with the waves and the currents, the sound and the fury.

You asked me, by the way, if this work about valuing the human has any political implications. I think you have answered your own question. The concept of the individual is so familiar that its political significance is overlooked. In the Middle Ages, there was little idea of people having their own interests or personal and unique identities. The same is true of many parts of the world I have seen on this journey that for now has come to a full stop.

Arguably, it was an ethic of valuing the human that drove the political agenda towards change in the West in previous eras. Whether you can make a case for that, the Protest against devaluation definitely contains the seeds of new thinking or a re-grouping of the existing agenda. I am convinced now you can't understand contemporary life without some concept of the struggle to realise our value. Social evils are a multiplication of layers of different forms of devaluation. The major challenge we have to face head on is the conversion of people into objects. This crops up everywhere and seems to be endemic in the human condition.

The good news though is that it can go into reverse. The torturers working for Saddam Hussein had been trained by the East German Stasi, who had in turn been trained by the Gestapo. This is a virus for dehumanisation transmitted around the globe. But, it also suggests that transmission of a healthy meme of valuing the human can be possible. So, I remain profoundly hopeful. It needs a critical mass, a people's covenant disbanding the old ways of dividing the world, grassroots initiatives rather than political statements and civil service replies.

I am optimistic. Acts of re-valuation take place all the time. Do you remember when the man from the council came to assess the property value of our house in Wiltshire? Dad argued that values had shifted, and we should have been paying less local tax. But, the re-valuation went the other way, and we ended up paying more.

I enclose a few chapters of a book I have been working on that tries to bring a map of how all this looks on the landscapes of our times. Please try to get it published. When I get out of here— and the man from the Embassy was hopeful the other day— we must go and have a drink together in Malmesbury and look up that old house.

Take care of yourself, and thanks again for doing what you did.

Matt

P.S. I'm pleased to hear that you and Liz went there together. And there's you saying you lack the patience to work at the constant negotiation that marriage requires!

44
Peaceweavers

Iphigenia, a Rwandan master weaver sits in front of her house, an hour from Rwanda's capital, Kigali, making beautiful baskets with her friend, Mukanyndwi. Her husband and five of her children were hacked and clubbed to death by marauding Hutu militias. Among her family's killers was Mukanyndwi's husband.

"In my heart, the dead are dead, and they cannot come back again," said the master weaver of those she lost. "So, I have to get on with the others and forget what has happened."

Four hundred Hutu and Tutsi women work together, weaving baskets for peace as part of Rwanda's rebuilding efforts after the devastating 1994 genocide. After the genocide, Rwandan women had been widowed by the thousand, left without any economic means of support. Now local women were creating sustainable enterprises, adapting traditional handmade goods for export to North America.

Using their income, Rwandan weavers were now purchasing food, medicine, and clothing, pay school fees, and open savings accounts. Along with a regular salary, the business was bringing reconciliation between victim and perpetrator. It was always hard to turn round and begin to work against patterns that moulded people. Difficult but not impossible, otherwise no one could ever dare to be different and get away with it.

It was a picture along the corridors of his memory guaranteed to raise a shout of hope in anyone's vocabulary, Peaceweavers weaving peace from the warp of indifference and the woof of difference.

45
The Last Trump

Dear Daniel,

It meant so much to get your letter. Brought tears to your Dad's eyes it did! And it sounds as if you're doing all right, beginning to get things back on track. I know Aunt Mandy has been a great help, but it's you that is doing the work. What pleases me most is not just that you are holding down a job and even got a promotion, but that you are starting to believe in yourself and value yourself. You said how much you had felt like crap in the past. To power up your life is closely linked with the sensation of being somebody, heir to a fortune valued beyond price.

Things are not easy here, as you may imagine, but I'm coping. It helps that I'm neither in solitary nor in a crowded cell. My cellmate is from Australia, arrested on a drug's charge. Will is asleep, his face long and thin as if his head were compressed. He looks slightly odd, an impression compounded by an incongruous combination of designer jeans and an old sweatshirt.

His HIV virus developed into full-blown AIDS earlier than expected. It has come on quickly during the past six months. Sometimes, Will fears his mind is slipping. He is already experiencing constant diarrhoea, weight loss and tiredness. And he's often getting unwell, fighting for breath. But, the symptom I am getting concerned about most here is deterioration of the brain. Will has difficulty remembering the names of his family.

I have never before seen so clearly how much impotence feels like fear.

He says he is glad I'm here, as he doesn't want to die alone if he is not released. It would make anyone think about the big issues of life and death. I have been trying to think out the puzzle of feeling worthwhile and the protest that calls out in its absence. I need to tell you my thoughts, as it is the only way to stay sane, what with Will losing his marbles.

So many contemporary issues assume the inherent value of a human life. Concern for relationships, justice for the poor, the importance of personal life over the system, the fight against prejudice and the rights of the disabled: they're all built on the proposition that we should treat people properly, that there's something special about each of us. All that work I used to do facilitating meetings and encounters in the workplace depends on an atmosphere of mutual respect being engendered. The sheer disregard for human value is why ethnic cleansing in Darfur is so obscene. We instinctively feel that you shouldn't treat human beings this way, but we can't give any real reason why not. A baby is born, welcomed and duly patronised. But, try talking down to an adult or even one of Aunt Mandy's pupils; lack of respect becomes a stormy issue!

Tonight we sat here playing cards. Nothing complicated, as my education was deficient! Whatever I played, Will seemed to trump me. The early part of the evening, he won fair and square. It struck me, though: There we were, playing for small grubby stones from the floor of the cell, having a laugh that was more than just an act of defiance. I don't think either of us had laughed so much for ages. By the sixteenth game, my losing streak was turned round and I began to get the measure of the game. I ended up trumping Will a good few times before we called it a night.

It set me thinking. What is the card that people play that so often seems to be a higher value than that of a human life? So often in my journey, the worth of people is trumped by causes and ideas. When in Russia, they wanted to rehabilitate someone like Stalin, the State power trumps the value of humans that are destroyed in such a system. The card of security and or a strong nation trumps most of the people most of the time. The terrorist who kills and maims for his cause— be it the pioneers of suicide bombing in Sri Lanka or those peddling their own political version of Islam— are trumping the people caught up in their acts. Victims don't come into it. They lie on the ground, not consulted, trumped by a higher value card.

African countries taking the side of perpetrators are allowing nationalism or anti-colonialism or whatever to trump the victims. Those are higher value cards just as we played when we were the masters out there. Those fanning religious persecution in Orissa in India or in Nigeria trump those they demonise. My cause shouts louder than your life. The suspicion of those caught up in community conflict trumps the value of some poor soul on the other side of the wall. The so-called freedom fighters, who assume the mantle of working-class (or anyone else's) heroes, are celebrating a cause that trumps the value of anyone caught in the crossfire. We can judge a system by how much it gives value to people or denies it. That holds good for capitalists and Caliphates alike.

How is it that anyone attracts support through acts that desecrate others so as to make a point? It's always the passers-by that catch the force of the fury. But, how come the constituency of the cheering values what the terrorists or war criminals have done more than the value of those that have been ripped up? The card of the perpetrators will always trump the card of the victims. Cruel people trump the humanity of others in the name of virtue. Ponder these things until they make you speechless, and then shout for all you are worth! Get involved in this cause if you can.

Take care of yourself and hope the summer holiday plans work out for you.

Write again soon,
Dad

46
The Monks of Malmesbury

It was England's oldest hotel, a pressure-free zone, a four-star, four-poster hideaway that offered country pursuits for the initiated. From the terrace of the Old Bell Inn, an October evening sun daubed an entire landscape with a glow that was almost eerie. At times orange, at times green, the light gently sought out the true nature of things, lending every image sharper focus. On the green opposite, under the soft lights of the Abbey, several people were walking their dogs, enjoying the enthusiasm with which they ran to fetch the sticks that were being thrown in teasing, repetitive action. A pair of bull terriers were in a state of over-excitement, their high spirits making them belt round the green. Like lovers, they could not bear to be parted. One of them howled like a mad thing when the owner got hold of its friend and insisted it was time to go.

The eight-hundred-year-old Malmesbury Abbey had been a holy site for worshippers for centuries. It was the site of the tomb of the First King of England and, during the Middle Ages, housed a seat of learning to rival Oxford and Canterbury. A benefactor of the Abbey, William the Conqueror, lamented on his deathbed that he had not mixed zeal for religion with sufficient humanity. Malmesbury was constituted a Benedictine House, a Rule of Life renowned for hospitality. Aldhelm, scholar and priest, was appointed the first Abbot. Under his leadership, Malmesbury continued to be a seat of spirituality and learning in the realm.

King Alfred recorded an incident that sought to capture the spirit of the first Abbot of Malmesbury. Aldhelm used music, humour and riddles to encourage the people to take their faith more seriously. With sadness, Aldhelm observed that the peasants, rather than joining in the singing in church went about gossiping and couldn't be persuaded to come to the sermon. On the bridge in the town, Aldhelm stationed himself as a minstrel, singing popular ballads and telling stories. Soon, by the beauty of his verse, he had collected a crowd of hearers. When he had their attention, he gradually introduced more serious subjects. The chronicler William of Malmesbury observed that if "he had proceeded with severity and excommunication, he would have made no impression whatever upon them."

Benedictine peaceweavers abounded in those far-off times, many of them rooted in religious communities, skilfully combining the warp and weft of justice and human weakness into embroidered tapestries; teaching and learning the arts of peaceweaving so as to foster patterns of reconciliation.

The Saxon King Athelstan made a gift to the people of Malmesbury for helping them fight the Danes. They would have common ground southwest of the town on which to graze their animals, to play and use in perpetuity. It was called King's Heath. Subsequently, the common ground was translated into an allotment to be worked. [xvii] But, the gift was only for the local people. If they moved away, they were barred from that common ground, "discommoned," as it continued to be called.

What if Common Ground showed that what was primary about people was not just that they all came from somewhere and had an identity but that they shared a shining humanity that was realised in and through what they were, for this also defined them.

What if common ground were a gift, not just to one town or one group but to all people, and they could not be evicted from it unless they exercised an opt-out clause?

"Hurt not others with that which pains yourself." - Buddhism: Samyutta Nikaya V.353

"As thou deemest thyself, so deem others." - Sikhism: the Kabir

"Do not to others what, if done to you, would cause you pain." - Hinduism: the Mahabharata, Anusanana Parva 113.8

"No one of you is a believer until he loves for his brother what he loves for himself." – Islam: Fortieth Hadith of An- Nawawi 13

"What is hateful to you, do not do to your fellow man" - Judaism-Talmud: Shabbat 31a

"Always treat others as you would like them to treat you" – Christianity: Matthew 7:12

47
The Seven Glasses of Wine and the Seven Awakenings

It was his final message.

"There are seven cups and seven awakenings," said the Peaceweaver. "Life offers us seven glasses of wine. Without the last, experiences leave us dry and thirsty, as if we were drinking water bottled from the sea."

"What are these seven cups and the seven awakenings?" they wondered.

"The first awakening," he answered, "is the awakening to life. We find ourselves alive, a mystery to ourselves, adrift on an open sea. Everywhere extends the house we call self. Mothers, fathers, primitive comfort, primeval security, things, objects, the world: all blend, and where the boundaries begin and end, we learn in our first education."

"And the second cup?" they asked him.

'The second cup brings an awakening to the world of other people: brothers, sisters, school, college, clubs, friends. All break walls of the central citadel of self, forcing us to act, react, interpret, interact. To live is a course in unstitching a self-oriented life."

"The third cup brings an awakening to development and education, to realisation of who we are, of our potential, of our gifts."

"And the fourth cup?" they asked him.

"The fourth cup brings an awakening to the mysterious incarnations we call the opposite, as Adam stood before Eve and learnt to speak a new language. It is the cup of human loving, its highs and lows, its tragedies and its triumphs. Few have not tasted of this cup, its untramelled bliss and its despairing depths and sweet surrender."

"And the fifth?" they asked. "What's in the fifth cup."

"The fifth cup is the awakening to career, to work, to the significance of significance and be someone, someone who counts, who is needed and who can contribute gifts. Without the awakening that comes with this cup, many lives are a song unsung. And those expelled from significance find that the dregs of this cup can be bitter indeed."

"The sixth is the cup of reflection. The awakening to beauty and making room for the things of the spirit and of creativity. A cup of parenthood and grandparenthood, of making something that will be more important than we are, that will outlive us."

"So what is the seventh cup and the seventh awakening?" They were curious.

"The seventh cup is the cup of life-giving water offered to all who acknowledge their thirst. It is an awakening to the source of our value, the essence of our worth and where that is lodged."

"There is," said the Peaceweaver, "a cry at the heart of things, a sob of anguish wrenched and torn from human life. A planet is in pain like a jagged peak rising with unbowed contrast amidst gentle hills, an abrasive surface where to rub the hands brings sharpness and discomfort."

"We live in a land of such contrasts, where gentleness and jagged roughness live side by side and where beauty and pain are intertwined, for the world is abrasive to the human spirit and to rub against others is to reel with the discovery of an unexpected sharpness. Amidst the good and the kind, how did the blue and white planet become a scene of torment, a world carved out of an inhospitable wilderness, so friendly to human life, so unfriendly to itself?"

It was the question that had haunted him since sitting in that tree all those years ago, watching the late-night dance of the stars. "Is there anything out there that corresponds to what's in here?"

"Your life here is determined by what you think is out there, the conditioned by the unconditioned, the temporal by the timeless, the imperfect by what is perfect, the changing by what is changeless. We are built to measure our thinking and acting by what is greater. Or will we be as those who derive their own measurement out of themselves? Within us all, there is song waiting to be sung. As butterflies are drawn by the light, so you are drawn to the greater against which you to test your life; you are in search of it; you cannot escape from it. There is a room that is never empty. It is the dimension of faith, of our ideals, of a realm larger than us to which we must pay homage. No more can we rid ourselves of what we think is ultimate than remove from our minds length, breadth or height; past, present or future."

48
A Letter of Resignation

Dear Mandy,

    Thanks so much for your letter. It meant more to me than I know how to say. By now you will have resumed school again after a long summer holiday. I hope you have a really good term. You are one of my heroes… or heroines I should say!
    Across the dimly lit corridor, there are a couple of Burmese men arrested for robbery. From what I can make out, they keep re-iterating how unjustly they were imprisoned. It's curious. When it affects them, even thieves expect to be treated fairly. We tear up agreements and treaties but expect contracts to be kept in return. If we do not subscribe to fair and kind behaviour, why expect it from others?
    Once, there was a prisoner in solitary confinement. He was so desperate for community, he responded to his enforced isolation by making imaginary friends. With them, he would take turns to play, talk, fight and respond. But there was a problem. The responses of his companions were always based on his own previous experiences. Surprise, novelty and challenge were always lacking. "A decent conversation with oneself is after all impossible," the prisoner concluded before he hung himself. Those who have a poetic conception of solitude couldn't stand complete isolation, not even for a whole day.

Now it is three in the morning. For some reason, I can't bear the thought of another night coming on. I will cheer myself up with better stories than this.

Tonight my cell is silent, silent with early morning intensity. I am glad not to be isolated though I'm not sure how much longer my cellmate has.

I think a great deal about the past. An odd experience once happened to me in which I had for an instant, pushed the button on my own landline number, which then recorded that I had been phoned. Checking to see what the last number was and re-dialling, I had the strange sensation of talking to myself: a circular internal conversation, the laugh of an empty horizon. I think I now see through the emptiness of the mood I had willingly embraced, a spirituality rising and falling into itself, consumer religion to help the soul understand its own inner workings.

I hope and pray that a movement of ordinary people is gathering pace to set a new course for the twenty first century, where in this globally connected world, we cannot afford for a year more, the luxury of not so splendid isolation. Sooner or later the regime here must come to understand that.

But, I am tired of trying to save the world. Everything is a failure. No one is listening. Maybe it's this partially lit cell affecting my judgement but I am all too keenly aware of my own shadows to be totally at home in a world of light. The truth is I have moved successfully across a landscape of devaluation, especially where Sara was concerned. When Sara and I were first in love, we were smitten. There came a blinding light and we were lit up, as if a thousand flashlights had fixed on target. We were transfigured, unsustainably faultless until moments of let down inevitably occurred. We glimpsed something extraordinary about each other. It's our true value we caught sight of, a view from above, a sweet shining of each other in a distant mirror. Now I have to live with the truth that we are not just the hunted. We are also hunters. Me- I'm a hunter!

It is now four in the morning. I need to ask your forgiveness for our action that led to Dad's death. How that has shaped your life as well as mine! I see as if five minutes ago the day your grief turned to anger. 'If it wasn't for you running off like that....." Until that India trip and the many conversations we had together, your words had shut me up in a sealed room, unable to talk about it since or resolve the guilt that had hounded us like stubborn dogs for thirty five years.

The past does have an irritating habit of catching up with you. Too much has happened. The seeds we've sown are ripening for harvest. So what with my regrets about yesterday and today not having been brilliantly successful, that only leaves tomorrow.

Last night it was there before me once again, the thirty centuries, or was it only thirty seconds, before the explosion. Dad's face looking at us boys for half a lifetime, willing them to live though he would not. For a long lingering eternity, we looked at each other, the sacrifice and the freed, rescuer and rescued. Absorbing the fatal impact, Dad dissolved into a living flame, the sacrifice wholly consumed on the altar. He knew that if he took the blast, we would be all right.

That has helped me years later to come to terms with it. Until recently, 1 knew I must go on refusing absolution. To be let off the hook would be cheap at any price. Better to wander the world, a fugitive, cut off from the show that everyone else seemed to be enjoying so heartily. From being known as the Peaceweaver, I am now stepping down and coming to peace in that interior landscape of a restful heart. It's great to imagine a day when silent dignified mass protests will signify that people everywhere are rejecting the old patterns of devaluing and weave an alternative future. It's even greater to see small steps along that road as people change things, one garden at a time and realise this is actually happening and it's no dream.

Once I was bent on exploring a new vision of the universe. Matter, space and time would never be the same again. It seemed to chime in with an eastern mindset, the Tao of physics, everything interconnected in a dance of energy. That way of thinking still has an appeal but then I come back to the event that defined my life for a long while. I had convinced myself that matter has far less substance than everyone thought. But I couldn't deny that Dad had been pulled apart by something solid. The real world was substantial enough to take him.

I had thought reality was far too superior to be expressed by words. But I couldn't get away from the propaganda of those who seemed to crow over Dad's death. For me, it undermined all that post-modern thinking everyone is imbibing these days. In the real world, words mattered, distinctions counted. Truth and falsehood involve real differences. The rage I allowed myself to feel showed me that truth needed to be brought out into the open. Until Steve went to see the family, I knew I ought to forgive though it still felt it let them off the hook. Those times have remoulded my life.

Here we are, children of the permissive age, raised amidst the distinct tremor of social and moral earthquake and the crumbling of values and institutions. Maybe it's the prison cell getting to me. But I can't side with those who convey an easy familiarity with the cosmos. I want to stand awe-struck before everything that is beautiful. I want to cease living in a drab, functional world drained of astonishment. Just as once I was tired of a sardonic rationalism and the materialism that had blighted my life, so now I'm tired of the props being the centre of the stage. There has to be more. I'm a person, I hurt. I wasn't going to tell you this but you might as well know. I may not have long to live. But is there any echo? Does the universe respond to my cry to count, to be conscious, to be loved and valued? Or is all our humanity met with a cruel mocking laugh, like... like the laugh of an empty horizon?"

So many travellers on the journey of life exhaust themselves on the senseless pursuit of material possessions and finish without finding spiritual capital. There comes a point of muddied realisation that the road will not be so long as we first thought. The journey will soon be over and all too soon we start asking ourselves what will be our legacy to the next generation. But there are travellers who seek healing from the pain of life and the baffled perplexity that haunts us all, for whom the answer lies in a difficult trip back to the beginning of the journey.

Your own journey has brought you integration. But maybe I am starting to understand mine. It has come to a halt yet, strangely the journey continues.

I remember that pony Dad bought you. Was Duke his name? I can't recall exactly. But I see you riding off and pausing to pick the bud off a tree that hung limply besides the footpath. Galloping days; galloping, galloping, galloping, days, the steady, heady rush of time enabling us to stand outside of ourselves; to look back and look ahead.

Strange considering where it led me, but I have always had an adventuresome streak. So I am ready to go on ahead and see what it is round the next corner.

Please look out for Daniel till I get back. What you've done for him is redeeming.

Lots of love,
Matt

49
The Return of the Human

Early on the first morning, before the world stirred, the Peaceweaver left the house. The old woman had left the imprint of her presence everywhere.

A month had passed. The morning after the night of despair had been a blur of bewildering scene changes— the key in the lock, the man from the prison, the man from the embassy, a hurried goodbye to his compulsory roommate, the intensity of the light, coffee with the ambassador and a drive to the airport. Then had come the long flight home, and amidst the press and the fluorescent glare of publicity came the hugs and a welcome from family that took his breath away. Liz and Steve, Mandy and even Daniel— especially Daniel— stood there as large as life itself. That night, the wine flowed, congratulations flowed, and well-wishers endowed him with smiles.

But, Mandy and Steve had news for him. Aunt Freda had died two months before. After time spent with Daniel, who was navigating his way to a rich seam of personal worth, Matthew knew he had to visit the home where his own boyhood had been put back together. They all came.

Her cottage was much like he remembered it, except its central soul was gone. But, the tree with all its branches was intact, the tree on the hillside outside the cottage where he used to look up at the stars.

From having been awash with a million impressions, his world was glued back together, and now he understood the journey. For these past ten years, he had listened to the music of the world, matching its themes against the sounds he was hearing from within him. But, until that dark night in a Burmese jail, he had never realised those songs could harmonise and blend together. He felt that at a profound depth, he mattered, and with that knowledge, the song was returning, an integrated song, a story set to music with a beginning, middle and an end. To a world that aspired to be holistic, he now knew of a single story, a finished symphony that could impart the waning gift of coherence.

His journey had taken him through many towns and cities. He had spoken about the value of a unique soul in front of audiences that yawned with indifference, audiences that were hostile and before audiences that were open. In market places, in village halls, in larger auditoriums, wherever he could gain a hearing and the people gathered, he told his story, the story of the conversion of humans into objects and how it was possible to re-image the landscapes so that the conversion process could be reversed. The story he told was not to him a mirage or a fiction or a pleasant and idle tale signifying nothing. He had felt its power. His own depths had been transformed by it. And even while he was in prison and unable to influence anything, people had caught the vision. Momentum was clearly growing. Common ground was increasing.

He looked out. It was gently raining. Soft rain bathed a whole landscape. The rain did not deter him from walking towards the familiar footpath to the sea. His footfall made a quiet echo on the hillside. Up a little, further along, past rows of hedges and at the top of the hill, the walker paused to draw breath and take in the scenes that begged to be described and felt. Painters and photographers had been drawn here to capture the soft landscape and offer it to others for view— splashes of yellow seed amidst greens and brown. How many types of green could there be?

As he continued his walk, he felt a pang for the lost years consumed by midges that gathered here in the summer months. Time had defined the point at which he started the journey. Through the inscrutable power of time, the inhabitants of Earth were able to distance themselves from themselves without fear of becoming disjointed.

By now, he had reached the seashore, something made the seagulls and cormorants screech at one another above his head and then they fell silent. The action of the waves had been turbulent that night. Wind and waves had formed an incredible array of shapes and patterns in the shifting sands.

"What is this journey we find ourselves making with companions on the road?" he wondered. "Is there is a supreme power guaranteeing a unity in things and a direction to events, a single story making sense of the impotence and vulnerability of existence and the Protest we hear from within? Is there anything out there that corresponds to what's in here?"

"Listen to the music," Aunt Freda had instilled into him.

What was his vision of the world? What had he learned in ten years of wandering, wondering, questioning, and curiosity without ceasing, marvelling at the source of wonder, examining the reason for his questioning and intrigued by his own curiosity?

If his journey had taught him anything it was how we could weave a tapestry of peace out of the unpromising warp of difference and weft of indifference. The plane crash wreckage across the human landscapes of time needed not be the last word or the final battle. Why could it not happen that people were more committed to the challenge of peaceweaving, resolving their battles in a way that brought winners because the concerns under the surface of the deep were being heard. Increasingly, agendas and campaigns and battles that had been fought on different fronts were being regarded as fighting on common ground. After the collapse in economic value had washed over the world, was it his imagination that human stock was rising in the market places of the times? Realising the problem, in villages, small towns, and big cities, citizen's unions, community organisations, and faith congregations were adopting resolutions and taking practical steps promising an end to the old dehumanisation. Local people were offering food to their neighbours, getting to know them as people, especially those they wouldn't naturally like because they were not like them. Why should these things not be so?

Even as he imagined a world invaded by possibility, there came deeper questions relentlessly forming and breaking like the wind-tossed waves across the beach.

He wanted guidance. "Show me," he asked. "What is the mystery of my humanity? The world is vast" (for he had now spoken in five continents) "but there is a universe within. Why am I a mystery to myself, reaching for the stars but condemned to fall back? Who is this riddler who even asks the question?"

The sea beckoned. He walked towards it. Still it beckoned and called, at first whispering then with gathering intensity. He plunged in, feeling the cool water rushing at him. He felt like he was part of everything, connected, immersed in it all, rejecting the separateness that keeps us doing terrible things to each other.

Behind him, there was a shout and cheering as his family had caught up with the solitary walker and were following suite, plunging in with zestful abandon.

Then he heard again a wave gently breaking upon an eternal shore. And there came to him a time of revealing, a stream that flowed and glistened in the running living shining of the sun. He felt he was experiencing a kind of death in which the soul left the body, the soul of him separating from the confines of bodily material existence and then leaping, exulting from its prison and soaring, soaring into the clear limitless sky and sea. In that time of the rising of spirit, sight was given to him, eagle sight that saw over the range of things.

The whole world had changed for him. He had glimpsed a moment, a moment when real peace between people would no longer be sidelined as flimsy and utopian but become the sturdy material of practical everyday weaving. He had witnessed a time when the conversion of objects into humans had ceased, the machinery spiked, the process reversed. An inward cheer exploded into a shout that broke surface as the birds screeched in agreement and the emerging sun celebrated the return of the human.

POSTSCRIPT
The Fiftieth Chapter

"The human and physical worlds are so interconnected, both within themselves and within each other, that everything can be said to affect everything else. We are inter-related beings in an inter-related world."[xviii]

"People slide by degrees into doing things they would not do if given a clear choice at the beginning. Each of the early steps may seem too small to even count, but later anxiety about the moral boundary may only suggest the uncomfortable thought that it has already been passed."[xix]

50
The Year of Jubilee

In a village long ago, there lived two children who were brother and sister. They were mischievous children who enjoyed playing pranks, much to the annoyance of those around them. Outside the village, there lived an old man who had a very different kind of reputation, a reputation for being wise and for being a weaver of peace.

The two children decided to play a trick on him.

"We will go the wise man," said the brother, and we will pose a riddle, a riddle that cannot be solved. And we will say, 'We have caught out the wise man!' "

"Let's catch a butterfly," said the sister suddenly. "And we will take it to the wise man. And we will say to him, 'O wise man, O wise man, is the butterfly in my hands dead or is it alive?'"

"And if he says, 'It is alive,' we will crush the butterfly," the brother said. "He will be wrong."

"And if he says, 'It is dead,' we will open our hands, and the butterfly will be released," said his sister. "Either way he will be wrong, the spell of his reputation broken." That is how, a few days later, the two children searched out the old wise man and explained that they had a question that needed answering.

"Tell me," asked the wise man.

"O wise man, O wise man," began the sister, "my brother has a butterfly in his hand. Can you say if it is dead or if it alive?" The wise man thought and thought. And he thought and thought. "It is," he said after a while, "in your hands!"   - Source unknown

[i] Zeldin, T. (1998), An Intimate History of Humanity. London: Vintage Books, p. 143
[ii] Baudalaire, C. (1964) The Painter of Modern Life and Other Essays. Oxford: Phaidon Press
[iii] www.gatesfoundation.org/AboutUs July 2008
[iv] Du Boulay, S. (1988) Tutu: Voice of the Voiceless. London: Hodder and Stoughton, p. 61
[v] Stephenson, P. (2002) Billy, London: Harper Collins, p. 44
[vi] Sana al-Khayyat (1990) Honour and Shame: Women in Modern Iraq. London: Saqi Books, p. 35
[vii] Ferguson, M.ed (1993) The History of Mary Prince, a West Indian Slave, Related by Herself. Ann Arbor: University of Michigan Press, pp. 60-63
[viii] London Independent. 10 June 2008
[ix] Tawney, R.H. (1953) commenting on his experiences at the battle of the Somme, from, The Attack and Other Papers, London, George Allen and Unwin
[x] Ziauddin Sadar London New Statesman June 2008
[xi] Nussbaum, M. (2004) Hiding from Humanity. Princeton University Press, Princeton NJ p. 247
[xii] Scheper-Hughes, N. & Bourgois, P. eds (2004) Violence in war and peace. Blackwell Publishing. Malden, MA, p. 11
[xiii] Volkogonov, D. (1994) Lenin: Life and Legacy. Tr & ed. H. Shuckman. London, p. 310
[xiv] Cowan, R. (2002) Guardian. 25 June 2002
[xv] New York Times October 29, 1995
[xvi] Glover, J. (2001) *A Moral History of the Twentieth Century.* London:Pimlico p38
[xvii] Moffatt, J.M. (1805) *The History of the Town of Malmesbury and of its Ancient Abbey.* Tetbury: J. G. Goodwyn
[xviii] Barker, C. (2003) Cultural Studies. London: Sage, p. 125
[xix] Glover, J. (2001) A Moral History of the Twentieth Century. London: Pimlico, p. 35

Lightning Source UK Ltd.
Milton Keynes UK
09 October 2009

144742UK00002B/2/P